MW01256705

SOMETHING GREATER IS HERE

KENNETH J. HOWELL

CHRESOURCES

CHResources
PO Box 8290
Zanesville, OH 43702
740-450-1175
www.chnetwork.org

CHResources is a registered trademark of the
Coming Home Network International

Printed in the United States of America
ISBN: 978-0-9907921-1-6
Library of Congress Control Number 2015933401

Cover design and page layout by Jennifer Bitler
www.doxologydesign.com

Table Of Contents

✠

Foreword

Never before in the history of the world have our lives been so inundated with opinions on what is best for us, for our families, and for our future. There no longer is one Bible, for there are hundreds, maybe thousands, of translations. There no longer is one Church or one religion, for there are thousands of denominations, religions, sects, and cults. There no longer is one gospel, for the number of permutations nearly equals the number of pulpits worldwide. There no longer is a simple, limited, manageable selection of trustworthy books and outlets for information, for there is instead a near infinite array of voices, growing exponentially every day.

The idea that something *more* is out there seems obvious and even trivial, for that is precisely all that there is: more and more, until our lives and the lives of our children and grandchildren become paralyzed by the myriad of voices, leaving our world and their world unsustainable.

Certainly around us are many who seem content in their corner of this "more and more," shutting their eyes and ears to any challenging variations, certain and content that they have found what is eternally true. Maybe you are one of those, certain that where you have always been and where you are now is precisely where you must stay with no need to budge!

But in the midst of this "more and more," how can you or I be certain that what we have found is indeed true, beautiful, and good? That what we have learned from infancy, have studied, maybe even taught, is the fullness of what is true, or merely a shadow that has been passed down and along from generation to generation unexamined?

If, through the love and mercy of God, there is something more out there — something greater — a gift offered by our

Creator to help us break through the cacophony of today's aimless din of nonsense — something different from what you have ever considered — would you be able to break free from the bonds of your present assumptions to hear, understand, and accept? And how would you determine whether this new gift is indeed true and trustworthy?

Well, there is such a thing, a gift; that is, there is such a Person. And He's not new, and His voice has rung true throughout the ages, piercing the confusion, surviving all suffering, and the community of His mercy and grace survives with Him, Militant, Suffering, and Triumphant.

There is something greater here, and it is here for you. This is what Dr. Kenneth Howell has come to share: his own personal search, from the comfort of his childhood religious inheritance, through the many sufferings of his life, through the joys of his journey of faith, through his determined study to clarify the confusions of modern Christianity, and, in the end, to the discovery of that which God offers to anyone who asks, seeks, or knocks.

It is my hope that Ken's candid account of his journey of faith will help you discover that there is indeed something greater here for you, too.

Marcus Grodi
Founder/President
The Coming Home Network International

✢

PREFACE

The Jewish leaders of Jesus' day asked Him to give them a sign of His being sent by God to do the things He did. He responded that the sign they sought was already here (Mt 12:41-42). He provided them with two great figures of Israel's history whom He knew they could not dispute: Solomon and Jonah. The first had been exalted to the throne of his father, David, and was honored by a royal visit from the Queen of the South. The second had been humbled for his disobedience but then honored by the repentance of the king and people of Nineveh. Both were lodged in the Jewish memory as signs of God's work in the world of men. Yet they also pointed forward to a time when an even greater sign would be given to God's people, the sign of God in human flesh. Something great was here.

If Solomon had been honored by the visit of a queen and Jonah had been honored by the repentance of a pagan city, Jesus' compatriots should certainly have recognized Him as greater than Solomon and Jonah. Something greater was there. Yet, even the presence of something greater does not ensure that people will be able to see and appreciate its greatness. I did not. Throughout my whole life, something greater was here, waiting on me to acknowledge it, but I failed to see it — not because of malice or obstinence, but because of ignorance and self-will.

Like all human pilgrims, I came to the realization that God is forever beyond the grasp of our minds. Yet, this same God can be known and loved by hearts willing to fall down before the mystery of His presence and grace.

I found that such a God is the end and purpose of life. Nothing less will do. Something greater, much greater, still awaits us in the Beatific Vision.

CHAPTER ONE

✛

THE BEGINNING OF MY SEARCH
FOR SOMETHING MORE

1952-1987

On the wall of my childhood bedroom hung a picture of a
clipper ship, one of those nineteenth-century vessels that
sailed the world to bring spices and artifacts back to America
and Europe. With their billowing sails and long slender hull,
those ships evoked something that has never left me. I imagined myself as a crewmember out to see the world, places far
away and little understood. I had a desire to go there to see
how other people lived and to understand a world very different from my own. I longed for adventure. And since the
boy is the father of the man, I still possess that spirit of adventure today. I have always had a sense that there was something
greater out there waiting on me, and I have always wanted to
be *there*, not here.

I was born and raised in Tampa, Florida into a Presbyterian
family not unlike most American families of the 1950s. I was
baptized as a baby on March 29, 1953 into the Protestant Faith
that had been part of my family for decades, maybe centuries.
That Presbyterian or Reformed Faith was lived out in Semi-
nole Presbyterian Church, the name taken from the Native
American Indians who once roamed this southern wilderness.
Tampa had been the birthplace of my parents and the long-
time home of both sets of grandparents. Our roots went deep
in the Florida soil. To me, snow was as foreign as China and I
frolicked in the warm waters of the Gulf of Mexico as a child.

My childhood was by and large a pleasant one with three siblings: an older sister, an older brother, and a younger brother. My parents were hardworking and caring. My father was in the insurance industry and my mother was a homemaker. Since my older brother was only about two years older than me, I naturally did everything with him. As he could always do things better than me, I grew accustomed to not being the best. And I didn't resent this for a moment; I just always strove to be like him.

While still a child, God began teaching me the reality and value of suffering. When I was about ten years old, my older brother and I were playing football on the street with some neighborhood boys. Playing the wide receiver that day, I jumped up to catch a pass thrown over my head. My brother jumped, too, in an effort to deflect the pass, but when he came down, his elbow struck me in the left eye. I keeled over in excruciating pain. No one knew at the moment how serious the injury was but after a few days I noticed that my vision had been impaired. Over the next year my mother and I would make weekly visits to the eye doctor as he tried to fix my vision. This turned out to be a blessing in disguise. The doctor was an active and open Christian. I can still remember him, my mom, and me praying together in his office.

Gradually, my double vision went away and my vision returned to normal. However, a new problem developed. Because the muscles that made my left eye look up were paralyzed, the muscles controlling my right eye tried to take over. This turned my right eye inward, leaving me cross-eyed in that eye. This was not a happy thing for a boy of eleven as it caused me social embarrassment as well. The doctor decided the condition was operable. I remember lying on the operating table waiting for the anesthesia to take effect when that kind doctor leaned over me and said, "Don't worry, Kenny, God is with you and everything is going to be all right." And thankfully, it was. To this day, whenever I look out on the world with these aging eyes, or at my lovely wife, or upon my children and grandchildren, I'm eternally grateful for the skillful hands of the doctor and the mercy of God. Little did I know that the doctor's words would be bannered over my life like a prophecy. The sense of God's presence in the midst of suffering would be something to which I would later return as an adult.

SPIRITUAL AWAKENINGS

When I was fourteen years old, something completely unexpected happened. Having been brought up in a good Presbyterian home, I believed in God because it seemed the most natural thing to do. But God was not yet part of my thought life or my daily actions. One day I was home sick from school, lying in bed, when suddenly a light seemed to fill the room. For some reason, I wasn't scared because the light seemed warm and inviting. Growing up in Florida, I was accustomed to at least three hundred sunny days per year, but somehow I knew deep down that this light was not the light of the sun. I don't recall any words or visions but I simply knew in my heart that God loved me. Looking back, I now recognize that, after baptism as an infant, this was my first of many conversions.

My second and more profound conversion took place before the last year of high school. This time the Spirit's work in me took a deeper hold on my soul. When I started that senior year, I knew I wanted to become a Presbyterian minister. Growing up in the Presbyterian church, this seemed the natural thing to do. Since I had been a mediocre student at best, no one, however, would have guessed that I was destined for an academic vocation.

That final year of high school was different. I didn't do much better grade-wise, but it was different for a totally different reason. I was teaching myself the Bible, theology, and New Testament Greek. I had such a hunger to know the Bible that I would take it to school to read whenever I could.

I had had an inkling that I possessed some ability with languages when I did well in tenth grade Spanish with little, if any, study. But with NT Greek I was motivated. I asked my minister, who like all Presbyterian ministers had to study at least some Greek, to help me learn. Once he put me on the path, there was no stopping me.

During those early days of reading the Bible, I had a simple, childlike trust in the Word of God. I knew this book was God speaking to me and I wanted to hear everything He had to say. For some reason, I fell in love with the book of Deuteronomy. I must have read that book at least twenty times during the year. This feat would serve me well in years to come, for it was in Deuteronomy that I found the covenantal structure of the Old Testament. As a young man struggling with the temptations offered by the world, I memorized and clung to James 1:3, "Count it all joy, my brothers, when you fall into various temptations for you know that the trial of your faith works patience." I knew that if I stuck with the Bible and prayer, I would be able to be victorious over sin.

During that final year of high school I also read a book titled *Through Gates of Splendor*. It was the story of Jim Elliot as told by Elisabeth, his young widow. In the early 1950s, five young American missionaries went to Ecuador to evangelize the Auca people who lived deep in the Ecuadorean jungles. Before going, Elliot had met and married a young Christian woman named Elisabeth Howard. This book and a companion volume, *Shadow of the Almighty*, portrayed a young man of courage and adventure who was willing to leave the comfort of the United States and to live for the sole purpose of telling others about Jesus Christ.

Elliot's spirit of trust in God and his visionary work captured my imagination. His independent theology did not really agree with my Presbyterian background, but I still imbibed his missionary spirit. Since I already suspected that I could learn languages well, becoming a missionary seemed like a natural calling for me. Being a Presbyterian, I wasn't about to do anything without consulting my elders. Fortunately, they all encouraged me in my missionary aspirations, but first I had to go to college and then to seminary.

But maybe the most significant gift of that last year of high school was that my mother and I became very close. We prayed together, discussed the Bible together, and talked of my future vocation. My mother was and remains today a woman of deep faith. It was at her suggestion that I looked into Covenant College. I will always be grateful for her godly example and for directing me to that college.

By the time I finished high school, I was ready for a great adventure. I had a strong sense that God was in control of my life. I knew that something was out there waiting on me.

COLLEGE AND SEMINARY

Covenant College is a small Presbyterian school perched on the top of Lookout Mountain overlooking Chattanooga, Tennessee. What a great place to study and to grow in my faith! All the usual courses, as well as further studies in the Scriptures, theology, and languages continued to confirm the call to ministry.

The greatest gift of my years at Covenant, however, involved a woman, for it was there that I met Sharon Canfield. Our relationship was on and off during the four years of college, and at times, I tried to put her out of my mind by dating other girls. In the end, however, I simply couldn't shake the sense that I should marry her. She had more doubts about me, many justified, but after graduation in the summer of 1974, we agreed that we were meant for one another.

That fall, while Sharon remained back in Florida, I went off to Westminster Theological Seminary in Philadelphia. Then, on December 21 of 1974, we exchanged vows in Coral Ridge Presbyterian Church, the largest Presbyterian church in the State of Florida.

Seminary was a wonderful time of learning and theological growth. The intellectual stimulation was exhilarating, but all during my college and seminary years, one problem plagued me: Christian unity. Around me were hundreds of different denominations and independent churches, which to my mind conflicted with Jesus' prayer that He wanted His disciples to be one (cf. John 17). One of my seminary professors seemed to confirm my worries when he openly confessed that division among Christians was a scandal. Recognizing the problem, however, was easier than finding a solution. At that time, I comforted myself with the common Protestant idea of the invisible church, which says that the one true Body of Jesus Christ consists of true Christians scattered throughout many churches. Presbyterians, Baptists, Methodists, and a thousand others may not be the true church *per se* but the members of the one church of Christ were in each. There may have even been members of the one true Church in the Roman Catholic Church, even though I was convinced that the organization was corrupt. I struggled without success to find a resolution to this issue.

In 1977 I graduated from seminary and within a few months was ordained a Presbyterian minister. From that time until 1988, I had the great privilege of serving two churches. Many things during this period helped me grow to know how good and merciful God is, allowing me to preach and minister in His name.

One particular sermon I preached, however, stands out as a harbinger of my future journey. I was preaching on Psalm 100, focusing on the words of verse four: "Enter into his gates with thanksgiving and into his courts with praise. Give thanks to him and praise his name." Since I longed for my congregation to understand the true nature of Christian worship, I asked them to close their eyes and imagine themselves in heaven with God. There they would find an innumerable company of angels, accompanied by all the Christian saints of past generations who had served God faithfully. Together the angels and saints would be united in an unceasing song of praise that lauded the King of kings.

I then asked my small congregation to imagine the roof of our little church opening up and this heavenly throng of angels and saints descending into our midst. This union of heaven and earth, I told them, was the essence of Christian worship. At the time, I had no idea that this understanding of worship was the Catholic Church's teaching on the Mass. Rather, I assumed that the only way for Christians to experience this kind of worship was for us to feel it deep in our hearts, which I was trying to initiate through my imaginative preaching. The kind words I received after the sermon passed quickly, for this experience and vision of worship passed on into the regular duties of my pastorate.

In the summer of 1982, my growing family moved to Bloomington, Indiana, where I took up doctoral studies in linguistics. There I became the pastor of a second Presbyterian church. One particular couple attending our new church expressed significant interest in my Bible teaching, and the wife developed a friendship with Sharon. When I visited in their home one evening, they told me that they were Catholic and that they had been going to Mass every week as well as attending our worship services. When I heard this, I responded by telling them that we Presbyterians were catholic, too. They were puzzled. I went on to explain that at the heart of the Protestant Reformation was the question, "Who are the true catholics?" I told them that I didn't reject the title "catholic" at all. In fact, I said it was the Roman Catholics who departed from the ancient catholic faith. I proceeded to give them the version of history that I had learned in seminary, that the purpose of the Reformation was not to break from the church but to bring it back to its original purpose of preaching the Gospel; that the first few centuries of Christianity were more like modern Evangelical churches than like the modern Roman Catholic Church. I then insisted that if they wanted to be true catholics, they should become Presbyterian, which is what I believed St. Paul and the other Apostles had taught. Calvinism, as one prominent Presbyterian theologian put it, was Christianity come into its own.

Like most of my seminary classmates and fellow Presbyterian ministers, I sincerely believed that we were catholic, and believed that I was following in the very footsteps of St. Paul in the line of true believers in the early Church like St. Augustine. I did not despise Church history; I honored it. Only later would I come to realize that what I honored was a Protestant version of that history. In my heart, I wanted to be a true catholic, but the beliefs in my head did not allow me.

Being a pastor matured me a lot but left little time or motivation to explore the unresolved questions of truth still plaguing me. During the academic year 1984-1985, I had had the opportunity to teach as a visiting lecturer at Reformed Theological Seminary in Jackson, Mississippi. As I worked towards completing my doctoral dissertation, I yearned for the privilege of preparing young men and women for ministry, as well as the opportunity for freer theological exploration. In 1987, upon completion and a successful defense, I received my Ph.D.

in Linguistics, and by God's mercy and generosity, was accepted back onto the faculty of this fine Presbyterian seminary.

CHAPTER TWO

What I Always Wanted:
Teaching in a School of Theology
1988-1992

My new title at Reformed Theological Seminary was Assistant Professor of Biblical Languages and Literature. When my family moved to Jackson, Mississippi in the summer of 1988, I was on top of the world. As we set up house in Jackson, I felt as if I was now ready to do what I had always wanted to do. I had learned a lot from being a pastor but I had always wanted to go into teaching. Even though my doctorate was not in theology, my linguistic studies had included advanced work in biblical languages. I began teaching Greek and Hebrew, and would soon add Latin for students who wanted to go on to a doctorate after finishing their Master of Divinity degree.

One of the unspoken rules of the faculty and administration of the seminary was to test a new professor to ensure that he was a good teacher. If he was, he was more or less free to teach whatever he wanted, as long as he also taught his assigned subjects. For me this was wonderful. After my first year, I always taught an overload. In my second year, I began teaching courses in biblical interpretation and by my third year I was also teaching electives in science and religion. These courses would all have an effect on the eventual trajectory of my spiritual journey.

FAITH, REASON, AND GALILEO

Since 1980 I had been a member of the History of Science Society collecting many books on the history of science in general and on Galileo in particular. The underlying reason was the search for an adequate understanding of faith and reason. I had been reading a number of biographies of Galileo and standard works on the Scientific Revolution (sixteenth and seventeenth centuries) of which Galileo was a central character. The received opinion in the popular mind was that the Catholic Church had persecuted Galileo for his belief in the heliocentric system. In some versions, this opinion viewed Catholicism and Christianity in general as anti-scientific and more broadly anti-intellectual. In my heart of hearts, I knew this wasn't right.

I began collecting and digesting more technical and specialized articles written by experts in this period of history. I discovered that my doubts about the received opinion on Galileo were on target. The Catholic Church in the Middle Ages had been a major force in the founding of medieval universities. For example, the University of Paris had been founded in the twelfth century as an outgrowth of monasteries in Paris. Almost all European universities in medieval times had four faculties: Arts, Law, Medicine, and Theology. All students had to study the Liberal Arts before being admitted to one of the other three (higher) faculties. Contrary to public opinion, I discovered that the Catholic Church had been a major force in education and learning in the Middle Ages.

My most important conclusion in the case of the Copernican theory was that it was not a battle between science and religion. The pattern of learning established in the Middle Ages was still in place in the time from Copernicus to Galileo. All the major astronomers of this period were Christians — after 1517 either Lutheran, Reformed, or Catholic — who would have affirmed the divine inspiration of the Scriptures. All subscribed to the Augustinian dictum that there could be no conflict between the truths of the natural world and the truths of Sacred Scripture. Most pursued astronomy *ad gloriam Dei* (for the glory of God). Johannes Kepler, by far the greatest astronomer of his time, was a Lutheran who wished to be a theologian. When he realized that he would spend his life doing astronomy, he declared with pride that God had made him "a priest of nature."

The controversy surrounding Galileo began about twenty years before he was born. When Nicolas Copernicus published his *On the Revolutions of the Heavenly Spheres* in 1543, astronomers embraced his heliocentric (sun-centered) system of planetary movements, especially at the University of Wittenberg where Martin Luther had been a teacher. As astronomers studied the new book, they became divided in their opinion as to its truth. Galileo, born in 1564, embraced it as physically true. In the 1580s and 1590s astronomers debated the merits of the Copernican system, including its compatibility with the Bible. During this same period, almost everyone believed that the Bible taught that the earth could not move. They cited texts like Joshua chapter ten, Ecclesiastes chapter one, and Psalm ninety-three, but they also thought that there were few, if any, good empirical reasons to believe in the motion of the earth.

According to the Ptolemaic-Aristotelian system, the earth stood at the center of the solar system with the sun encircling it on the third sphere out (after Mercury and Venus). Galileo, on the other hand, believed in the physical truth of the earth's motion. After Galileo constructed a telescope in 1609 and discovered the moons of Jupiter, mountains on the moon, and the phases of Venus, he became a scientific luminary overnight. He was warned, however, that these things did not prove the Copernican system to be true and that he should refrain from entering into the biblical-theological issues since he was not a theologian. When biblical objections to the heliocentric theory began to circulate in his native Tuscany, Galileo wrote a famous *Letter to the Grand Duchess Christina* in which he argued for the compatibility of the Copernican system with the Bible. In other words, Galileo did not believe that the new astronomy contradicted the Bible; it only contradicted certain interpretations of the Bible.

As the controversy began to gain force, the Congregation of the Index in Rome took up the matter. The purpose of the Congregation was to review potentially heretical books and, if they were found to be heretical, place them on *The List of Prohibited Books*. Of course, to people in the twentieth century, such a list appears like censorship, but I learned two important facts. One is that scholars who requested permission to read the prohibited books were given permission if it was relevant to their research. In other words, the *List* only served to protect unlearned people who might be led astray; it did not constitute an absolute prohibition. The second is that not all books placed on the *List* were treated the same. Those that were condemned wholesale were usually theological books, not scientific ones. In the case of Copernicanism, it was only those books that attempted to teach the compatibility of terrestrial motion with the Bible that were absolutely condemned. Copernicus's book *De Revolutionibus* was prohibited "until corrected." This meant that astronomers could freely use it, but the parts that taught, or seemed to teach, the motion of the earth, had to be expunged. In other words, the Church was not forbidding astronomy or science; it was guarding against what at that time it considered dangerous notions. Even this, however, seems outrageous to modern people but the historian's first task is to judge matters from the standpoint of the original participants.

On March 5, 1616, the Congregation issued a decree in which Copernicanism was judged as contrary to good philosophy (read natural philosophy or science) and heretical in theology. The latter was because they judged it to be contrary to Scripture. When Galileo was informed of the decision, he accepted it. He knew — and his subsequent research shows — that this decree did not prohibit him or any other astronomer from studying Copernicus or from developing arguments for the Copernican theory. He took it as meaning that he could not advocate the theory publicly.

When Pope Urban VIII gave him permission to write a book on the subject, he wrote *The Dialogue on the Two Great World Systems* and published it in 1632. Even though this book passed the censors in his native Florence and even in Rome, it was taken by his scientific and theological opponents as an occasion to accuse him before the Inquisition of violating the 1616 decree. The following year, in 1633, the Inquisition initiated proceedings against him. The question was no longer one of astronomy strictly speaking but of obedience to the previous decree. Three expert readers reviewed the *Dialogue*. The most substantial review was from the pen of Melchior Inchofer. He maintained that Galileo had advocated the Copernican theory and thereby violated the decree. Galileo was asked four times under oath whether he had ever held or did now hold to the Copernican theory. He denied it four times. He said that he did not hold it since the decree of 1616. Yet his book was evidence that he did intend to advocate the Copernican theory. In the end, Galileo was found guilty of "the vehement suspicion of heresy" and was sentenced to life imprisonment. The sentence was quickly commuted to house arrest. He returned to Arcetri (near Florence) where he continued his scientific work, publishing his greatest work of science in 1638, *The Discourse on the Two New Sciences.*

My study of Galileo and the problems he faced with the Catholic hierarchy forced me to conclude that neither the Catholic Church nor Catholic culture was anti-scientific. To my surprise, the scientific culture that Galileo worked in was suffused with Catholicism and his trial was a witness to the Church's belief in the compatibility of Scripture and science. Their disagreement was primarily over whether the Copernican theory had been sufficiently proved. Although other scholars may differ in their judgment, I had to conclude that the proof for the motion of the earth was not strong in 1633, the date of Galileo's trial, and certainly not in 1616 when the Copernican theory was proscribed.

The officials of the Church made a wrong decision with regard to the science involved but, at the time, they had no way of knowing this. Nor was it a decision that impugned the infallibility of the Church. It was a disciplinary decision. So, while their decision in 1616 was factually wrong, it was a reasonable judgment given the available evidence.

Furthermore, I was impressed with how these Catholic astronomers (e.g., Clavius), natural philosophers, and theologians (e.g., Bellarmine) were all committed to the pursuit of truth in nature. They were not, as they have sometimes been portrayed, stuck in a rigid Aristotelianism or medievalism. They were open to change but only according to the standards they were using at the time, something very natural in all science. All of this disposed me to think more positively of the Catholic Church as regards its view of faith and reason.

BIBLICAL INTERPRETATION AND
THE PROBLEMS OF *SOLA SCRIPTURA*

I have always taken my teaching responsibilities seriously. As taught in Scripture, "Let not many of you become teachers, my brethren, for you know that we who teach shall be judged with greater strictness" (Jas 3:1). Therefore, I thought long and hard about how I could know that it was the Reformed doctrines that were taught in the Bible and not those of other Christian traditions. As a pastor, I had to preach and teach the Bible quite regularly. I often spent many hours translating the Bible from Greek and Hebrew, and reading commentaries and other theological literature to understand the text of the Bible. All this biblical study was generally confined to an interpretative outlook that was given to me by my Presbyterian heritage. As a Presbyterian pastor, I was expected to defend the Reformed position on theological questions, so there were limits on what I could say. And frankly, I genuinely believed that the Reformed view was the best expression of Christian theology. Yet, in the back of my mind, I still had nagging questions as to whether I was being honest with myself. As a result, I did not limit myself to this one outlook, but often read different interpretations.

So, when I began teaching classes on biblical interpretation (hermeneutics), I resolved that above all I would be honest with my students and myself. I would interpret the Bible with an open mind and let the chips fall where they may. I did and they fell on me.

I began to realize two important things. First, Christians of widely varying backgrounds could agree on many teachings in the Bible. For example, if they paid careful attention to John 14:6, they all came to the conclusion that Jesus is the Way, the Truth, and the Life. All orthodox Christians could also agree on the basic truths of the faith as summarized in the Apostle's

Creed. This gave me great hope, as I expressed earlier, for some kind of unity among Christ's followers.

But I also came to a second important conclusion that I found terrifying. There was little agreement on the meaning of many important texts that were central to some essential doctrines of individual traditions. Traditional Presbyterians, for example, place a high emphasis on election, citing passages such as Ephesians 1:3-14 and Romans 8:25-29. On the other hand, Wesleyans don't ignore these passages if they are honest with Scripture. Rather, they interpret these same passages on election and predestination quite differently from Presbyterians. This in itself was no great discovery. Many people realize this. My earthshaking find was that there was no way to decide between these interpretations by reading the Bible itself.

I applied my background in the philosophy of science to the problems of biblical interpretation. The philosophy of science tries to find proper methods to arrive at truth in science; in essence, it is the same problem as hermeneutics, that of formulating a proper method for finding truth in theology. I needed to find a proper method of biblical interpretation that would show that Reformed theology was in fact the best expression of biblical teaching. Given that I, like all true Protestants, believed in *sola scriptura*, I had to find my method within the Bible itself since it was the final authority in our theological quest.

Building on years of personal reflection, I labored vigorously to formulate an adequate interpretative method by which I could affirm the biblical truth of Calvinist doctrines. Search as I might, however, I had to conclude that the Bible has no method for arriving at its own true teaching. A dilemma was forming in my mind. If the Bible was my final authority for faith and life and yet the proper interpretation of the Bible was not to be found in the pages of the Bible itself, where was this proper method to be found? From outside the Bible? If the method is outside the Bible itself, then the Bible is not the final authority for our interpretative method. At best, one could say that the Bible contains the proper content (theology) but not the means (method) for getting at that content.

In wrestling with these conundrums, I came upon the *Commonitorium* of St. Vincent of Lérins. What struck me most was that a fifth-century monk had actually addressed the very problem of interpretative diversity. Vincent said that the Church should choose its interpretations by three criteria: "what is believed always, everywhere, and by all." The criteria of antiquity (*semper*), universality (*ubique*), and consensus (*ab omnibus*) allowed the Church to draw the line between orthodoxy and heterodoxy. His method implied that the Church should always seek to be in continuity with the past, always seeking what belongs to the catholicity of the Church, and always desiring a unified faith.

Two important truths imprinted themselves on my mind. First, the application of these criteria should tend toward a unified Church rather than toward the seemingly endless divisions within modern Christendom. Second, Vincent was simply explicating the method that the Church had used from its earliest times to distinguish truth from error, orthodoxy from heresy. In studying the history of the Council of Nicaea, I had already observed that the bishops at the council did not merely appeal to Scripture as if it were sufficient to settle the question of Arianism. They rather appealed to Scripture and to Tradition, the latter being the consensus of the Church prior to their time.

The significance of the veracity of Vincent's criteria began having an affect on other aspects of my studies, such as the true meaning of the Lord's Supper. I was arriving at the conclusion that the Reformed Faith was mistaken in the content of its creeds and that the faith of the ancient Church was not Calvinism. By realizing that Vincent's words represented a long held method of doing theology, I also was beginning to realize that the method of *sola scriptura* was not historically justified.

Instead of *sola scriptura*, I began to speak of *prima scriptura* (Scripture First) and *historia Christiana* (Christian History). By this, I meant that we should begin with the Scriptures but that we should read them through the eyes of the historic Church. In a sense, I had always been doing that inasmuch as I read the Scriptures through the confessional standards of Presbyterianism. Only now I was beginning to see that the creedal standards of the Reformed Faith were out of accord with both the content of the ancient faith as well as its methods. I saw that the divisions of Protestantism were rooted in its hermeneutics.

Then an even more severe problem with my Reformed Faith emerged. The issue of private interpretation of the Bible struck at the roots of my Protestant view of the Bible and shook me to the core. From childhood I had assumed that God wanted me and everyone else to read the Bible and study it carefully so we could come to the truths found there. I recall having a conversation in high school with a visiting Baptist minister at our Presbyterian church. We discussed the issue of infant baptism versus believers' baptism because I was at a loss on how to resolve this issue. Wisely, he encouraged me to study both sides of the issue thoroughly and then to make up my mind. That was what I had always sought to do.

My seminary training reinforced this assumed right of private interpretation. Over time, however, I had grown to hold a softer form of this axiom than many more independent minded Evangelicals. My form of the principle was not the "Jesus and Me" kind of theology but more that the Bible represented the final court of appeal. I respected and employed as interpretive guides the creedal standards of Calvinism, such as the Westminster Confession of Faith or the Canons of the Synod of Dordt. In the end, however, I often repeated Luther's "here I stand; I can do no other" when appealing to the Scriptures as my final authority.

Now in my mid-thirties, however, I was working at a more sophisticated level, one which caused me to go even further down to the roots. I realized that most of my life I had worked on the assumption that God had given me the right to interpret the Bible as best I could. I began to look back in history for when the idea of private interpretation of the Bible arose. I didn't find it in the magisterial Reformers (Luther, Calvin etc.) though I could have missed it, but I did find it in English writers in the seventeenth century. The assumption that God had given me a right of private interpretation now seemed suspect.

Could the idea of private interpretation be justified on the basis of the Bible? I studied 2 Peter 1:20 which in the RSV reads, "First of all you must understand this that no prophecy of scripture is a matter of one's own interpretation." Although this verse has been translated a little differently in some versions, the Greek text spoke clearly enough for me. Peter says that Scripture does not admit of (*idias epiluseos*) "a private solution." Once this was embedded in my consciousness, it became clear that I had been working on a false assumption. Scripture itself denied me the right to interpret it in my own way. Confessional Protestants (Lutheran, Reformed) tried not to engage in individualistic interpretation since they had creeds, documents that were necessarily of public nature. However, this was always the tendency in Protestantism. It was always a danger lurking just outside the walls of Protestant churches and which explains the proliferation of Protestant denominations. I did not yet know the answer but the problem was crystal clear. The idea of a living Magisterium in the Church was foreign to me but I inched toward it bit by bit.

I had come to Jackson and Reformed Seminary with the hope that I could remain there for the rest of my life doing what I enjoyed the most: teaching and research. It was gradually dawning on me, however, that my studies in both the history of science and Christianity as well as biblical interpretation were leading me away from Reformed assumptions. To my chagrin, I slowly was seeing that the Catholic Church had always had a great respect for human reason and for the public nature of truth, and it was truth that I wanted above everything.

✠

CHAPTER THREE

FROM THANKSGIVING TO EUCHARIST
DUC IN ALTUM
1990-1992

In 1990 I began teaching a course called Advanced Biblical Exegesis, and decided to have the students concentrate on one doctrine and study it in depth. The goal was to help them learn how to derive one major doctrine from Scripture, so that they could then do it for themselves later with other doctrines. But which doctrine? Which doctrine was most important for future ministers in a local church setting? The answer was clear. I had long thought that most Presbyterian ministers were at sea in their celebration of the Lord's Supper, not knowing exactly what should be done or why. Though many seemed to think that this sacrament was important, it nonetheless played a minor role in weekly church life. If I could make a contribution by having my students learn more about this sacrament, the effort would be worth it.

I designed the course in three sections: biblical exegesis, history of doctrine, and theological formulation. First, we studied the biblical foundations of the Lord's Supper by translating from Hebrew and Greek certain passages of Scripture pertaining to this celebration. These included the famous Passover narrative in Exodus 12, Malachi 1:11,14, and other Old Testament passages. Then we translated and read commentaries on the four passages in the New Testament that relate the institution of the Lord's Supper: Matthew 26:17-30, Mark 14:12-26, Luke 22:7-23, and 1 Corinthians 11:17-33. Finally, we studied other passages that are crucial to understanding the meaning of the sacrament: 1 Corinthians 10:14-17 and John 6: 25-59.

In keeping with my belief that the history of Christian doctrine was vitally important in theological formulation, I had my students write reports on various figures in the history of the Lord's Supper. So, beginning with the *Didache*, Ignatius of Antioch, Irenaeus, and Justin Martyr, we read what the first few centuries of Christian thought had to say about the sacrament. We went on to the Medievals and to the Reformation debates on the presence of Christ. Many Protestants think that the central issues of the Reformation were *sola scriptura* and *sola fide*, but just as or more important were the issues of the meaning and power of the Lord's Supper. This was as true for Protestants as it was for Catholics. In fact, the Lutherans castigated the Calvinists about the Lord's Supper more than they did the Catholics. We then read right up into the twentieth century, including Pope Paul VI's encyclical *Mysterium Fidei* (1965). Over the course of two years I felt myself slipping away into views inconsistent with Reformed theology. That process, I learned later, was really one of falling in love but I tried desperately to salvage my Calvinism.

REVIEWING AND REJECTING
JOHN CALVIN'S VIEW

I had long known that the Greek word for thanksgiving was *eucharistia* and that it was never used in the New Testament in referring to the sacrament of the Lord's Supper. I also learned in the course of my teaching that the word had quickly become a technical term for the sacrament under the influence, among others, of Ignatius of Antioch. At first, this fact alone was sufficient to show me that the early Church did not always retain the signification of Greek words used in the New Testament. However, I was content in my assumption that it was the Reformed tradition — and Protestantism in general — that had retained the biblical designation of the sacrament, as Paul uses the term "Lord's Supper" in 1 Corinthians 11:20. I was confident that as we explored the biblical roots of the sacrament, we would be confirmed in our conviction that the Calvinist position was the correct one, the one that most accurately reflected the teaching of the New Testament.

Among Reformed Christians, however, there were slightly different views on the presence of Christ in the Supper. The view most widespread among American Evangelicals was that of Ulrich Zwingli, the founder of the Reformation in Zurich, Switzerland: that the Lord's Supper was a pure symbol in the modern sense of an arbitrary representation of something else, much like a stop sign. In this view the bread and wine used in the Lord's Supper were always and only bread and wine. Christ's Body and Blood were only in heaven and would never return to earth until He personally returned to consummate world history and the kingdom of God. The Christian simply remembered Jesus' death on the cross and meditated on its saving power while participating in communion.

The other view was Calvin's. As the magisterial reformer of Geneva, Switzerland, John Calvin held that the Lord's Supper was a true sacrament, a true means of grace, and an important part of the Christian life. He was, however, very careful to distance himself from both the Roman Catholic view as well as that of Luther. Calvin argued that communion in the Holy Supper was indeed a true communion in the Body and Blood of Christ but not because Christ was somehow present in the bread and wine. It was a true communion because the Holy Spirit acted as a conduit between heaven and earth so that, while the believer on earth received only bread and wine in his mouth, his soul was feasting on the Body and Blood of Christ located in heaven.

When Calvin began writing *The Institutes of the Christian Religion* in the early 1530s, he tried to find a middle ground between pure symbolism associated with Ulrich Zwingli and the realist view associated with Luther. He agreed with Zwingli that the bread and wine were always and only bread and wine but he also insisted on something special about the Lord's Supper. It was Christ's gift to feed the souls of the elect by giving the essence of Christ's Body and Blood from heaven through the ministry of the Holy Spirit. The most important aspect of Calvin's teaching may be termed *receptionism*. He maintained that only the elect truly receive the Body and Blood of Christ. Unbelievers, even if they think of themselves as Christian, never partake of the Body and Blood of Christ. The Catholic Church and Lutheranism both taught what could be called the *manducatio impiorum*. Because Christ is present in the sacramental species apart from one's belief or non-belief in His presence, anyone who eats the bread and drinks the wine is eating and drinking of Christ whether he is a true believer or not. No compassionate pastor in any of these churches would attempt to judge who the true believers in their churches were but they would all acknowledge that not everyone who professed Christ was necessarily a genuine believer in the truest sense (cf. Mt 7:21-22). Catholics and Lutherans both insisted that all who partook were partaking of Christ. They did so to preserve the integrity and reality of sacramental doctrine. But Calvin would have none of that.

There was a strong connection between Calvin's view of election and predestination on the one hand and his view of the sacrament on the other. His receptionist view of the Lord's Supper grew out of his belief that it is only the elect in whom God works. Hence, Calvin says that it is only the elect who receive the Body and Blood of Christ through the agency of the Spirit. Unbelievers, the non-elect, who are members of the Church but not true believers in their hearts, never receive the Body and Blood of Christ. This view, of course, was at complete odds with the Catholic view that properly consecrated bread and wine become the Body and Blood of Christ after consecration.

THE LORD'S SUPPER IN THE NEW TESTAMENT

All these views on Christ's presence in the elements of the Lords' Supper claim to be based on the New Testament. How can one decide between them from the New Testament evidence? I needed to see the sacrament in the wider context of God's dealing with His people through salvation history.

At the same time as my class on the Lord's Supper, I was also teaching the Old Testament prophets. One of the major themes of the Jewish Scriptures was an emphasis on the presence of God coming to dwell with His people. The prophets of the Old Testament often pictured salvation in the messianic age as a second Exodus with the imagery of the pillar of fire and with the glory of God (*kabod*) dwelling in the midst of His people (see Is 4:5,6; Zech 2:5). The meaning of the original Passover and its renewal in the future days of the Messiah is summed up in the promise to Abraham, "I will be . . . a God to you and your descendants after you" (Gen 17:7). This promise stands at the center of the Old Testament promise of salvation that we have inherited. Prophet after prophet reiterated it. Isaiah especially announced the Immanuel theme in 7:14 ("the virgin shall conceive and bear a Son and shall call his name Immanuel") and declared the supremacy of the Messiah in chapter 9, verses 6-7. The promise of God dwelling with His people pervaded the prophetic hope. A century later, Jeremiah placed at the center of the new covenant this expectation: "I will be their God and they shall be my people" (Jer 31:33). Within a few years, the exilic prophet Ezekiel promised a new heart and a new spirit for God's people. Again, the renewed relationship was at the heart of his message: "I will be your God and you will be my people" (Ez 36:22-32). Lest we think that this promise of God's presence and person living in and among His people was limited to the people of Israel, the prophets teach that in the day of God's renewed covenant, the borders of God's love will be pushed back and all nations will be invited to God's holy mountain (Is 2:1-5). The former enemies of God's people (Egypt, Assyria) will now be counted among God's holy people (Is 19:18-25).

As I studied and then taught this dual background of expectations for the messianic age, I began to realize how much this pointed to a belief in the real presence of the Messiah as well as the catholic nature of the Church. The Church must be universal to fulfill the message of the prophets and God must really dwell among His people to satisfy all that was lacking in the first covenant.

The teaching of the New Testament builds on this background with its emphasis on salvation being a new experience of the presence of God. The act of God's Son becoming a man shows at once His humility and also His desire to be with His people. From the very beginning, in Matthew's account of Jesus' birth, the Immanuel theme of Isaiah pervades the story. The name Jesus, a Hellenization of the Hebrew name Joshua, means "the LORD is salvation," as the angel explains to Joseph (Mt 2:21). But salvation is explained further with the promise that God has come to be with His people. God living with His beloved people *is* salvation. Matthew's distinctive way of telling Jesus' life and ministry ends on the same theme of God's presence when Jesus tells the Apostles, "I will be *with you* until the consummation of the age" (Mt 28:20). Little wonder then that Jesus, in Matthew's account of the Last Supper, adds the words "*with you*" to His promise to drink the cup once again in the future fulfillment of God's Kingdom (compare Mk 14:25

with Mt 26:29). Jesus' ministry of salvation brought more than forgiveness of sins; He intended to give His own presence to His people as an eternal gift.

What form would that presence take? Would there be a renewal of the pillars of cloud and fire? Would He leave them a book to read so they might remember Him? Perhaps a letter would do? If they were careful and devout enough, they could probably muster the strength and courage to remember His ministry and continue it. But Jesus did not leave the problem of His continuing presence to the fickle powers of His Apostles. Nor did He leave them with a book or letter, though those would come in time. Rather, he gathered them together to do something each and every human being could understand. He gathered them for a meal and fed them. But this meal meant more than a time of fellowship and far more than a simple occasion of thinking on Jesus. Rather, Jesus transformed ordinary bread into His Body and everyday wine into His Blood. The words from His sacred lips, "This is my body," assured them that His own Person would continue with them in the Eucharist He had given them. He would not leave them orphans. He would be with them. Matthew's account of Jesus' life assures us that the Lord's Supper — the Eucharist — we celebrate today is nothing less than the presence of the same Jesus who first broke the bread that night long ago.

The real (bodily) presence of Jesus today is confirmed by the Greek word commonly translated "remembrance." The phrase "in remembrance of me" (*eis ten emen anamnesin*) occurs only in Paul's (1 Cor 11:23-26) and Luke's (Lk 22:19) accounts of the institution of the Lord's Supper. It is likely that Paul passed this down to Luke since they had close associations in ministry together. Unfortunately, our English word "remember" cannot do justice to the Greek *anamnesis* used by Paul and Luke. Our word "remembrance" suggests that we think about Jesus' life and death in our minds as an event that is in the past for us. There is no doubt that idea is included, but the Greek word means more.

Anamnesis means that the thing to be "remembered" is an otherworldly reality that is made present to the one "remembering." The past events of Jesus' life are taken up into the heavenly realms and are now made real to the worshiping community. Thus, when Jesus says, "do this in remembrance of me", He is calling on His Apostles to reenact that night. His assurance to them is that He will be with them in the future reenactment just as much as He was with them that first night. *Anamnesis* is not primarily a mental event on our part; it is a liturgical event on the part of Jesus' appointed representatives, the Apostles and their successors. We remember Jesus in our minds because He is here again just as He was to the Apostles — truly, really, substantially.

The bodily presence of Jesus on the altar underlies Paul's rhetorical questions in 1 Corinthians 10:16,17. These references to the Eucharist occur in a context of admonitions to avoid idolatry. Why should we avoid associations with false religions? Why should we not participate in pagan ritual? Paul's question in verse 16 assumes a powerful truth: "Isn't the cup of blessing that we bless a participation in the blood of Christ? Isn't the bread that we break a participation in the body of Christ?" The Corinthians already knew the answer to this question. Yes! This meal is a real participation, a genuine communion in the heavenly realities of the Body and Blood of Christ. The union with the one Lord excludes participation in the rituals of other gods. Paul explicitly confirms this: "you cannot drink the cup of the Lord and the cup of demons" (10:21). Such strong language is based on the belief that Paul had already passed on to the church at Corinth. This celebration so central to the life of the church involved a real communion with Christ.

I had come to realize that it was through the Eucharist that the presence of God promised in the Old Testament prophets was fulfilled, not once but innumerable times when the Church celebrates the Holy Sacrifice. On top of this, I saw that the traditional use of the language of sacrifice about the Eucharist, both in Scripture as well as in the writings of the early Church Fathers, struck at the very heart of the Reformation.

Both Luther and Calvin had denied that the Mass is a sacrifice. They claimed that to call the Eucharist a sacrifice was to denigrate the completeness of Christ's sacrifice on the cross. Yet, in the writings of some of the earliest Fathers, I encountered sacrificial language being used about the Eucharist. I discovered a text that I had never associated with the Eucharist, Malachi 1:11,14. In both the *Didache* and in Justin Martyr's *Dialogue with Trypho the Jew*, this text is cited as a support for the Eucharist being a sacrifice. Justin quotes it thus:

> My will is not among you, says the Lord, and I will not accept the sacrifices from your hands. Therefore, from the rising of the sun to its setting my name is glorified among the gentiles, and in every place incense and a pure offering is offered to my name because my name is great among the nations, says the Lord, but you defile it.

This showed me how the ancient Church had embraced the Catholic idea of the sacrament as a re-presentation of Christ's sacrifice on the cross. Here was more evidence that the Calvinist view lacked authority in the ancient writings.

EAT MY FLESH, DRINK MY BLOOD: JOHN SIX

With all that I had discovered, I still thought that the Real Presence of Jesus in the sacrament might still be understood in a spiritual sense as Calvin maintained. I had to return to the most disputed chapter of all, chapter six in the Gospel of John. On the surface, it is Catholics who seemed to take the chapter at face value. After all, Jesus calls Himself "the bread of life" (Jn 6:35,48) and promises eternal life through this bread: "This is the bread that comes down from heaven so that if anyone eats of it, he may not die." Even more strongly, Jesus says, "Unless you eat the flesh of the Son of Man and drink his blood, you have no life within you" (6:53). Then, not mincing words, Jesus states the matter plainly: "He who eats my flesh and drinks my blood has eternal life and I will raise him up on the last day" (6:54).

Many Reformed Christians insist that this chapter is about true faith and true communion with Christ, even of consuming Christ through faith but not in the physical sense that the Catholic Church believes. Reformed Christians often pride themselves on reading the Bible literally though this does not mean woodenly as many fundamentalists read it. For example, they do not insist that the days of Genesis One are six twenty-four hour days. They recognize that the Bible uses all kinds of literary metaphors and symbols. This less-than-literal reading of the Bible plays into the Reformed reading of John chapter six. They would note the presence of faith mentioned in the chapter. In 6:35, after calling Himself the bread of life, Jesus says, "He who comes to me will never hunger and he who believes on me will never thirst." And in verse 40, Jesus says, "Everyone who looks upon the Son and believes in him has eternal life." So, a Reformed Christian might think of the graphic language of eating the flesh of the Son of Man as a picture of true faith. In the same way that food is consumed in the body, so faith is the means of consuming Christ. They would insist, however, that this is not a physical eating the way the Catholic Church teaches. For them, the Catholic view borders on cannibalism.

It helped when I realized that the Catholic Church does not mean physically eating Christ's Body as a cannibal would consume human flesh. The doctrine of transubstantiation was articulated partially to eliminate such a misunderstanding. However, the Church insists that in the Eucharist, it is the true substance of Christ's risen Body that is consumed.

How could I decide between these two different kinds of reading of John chapter six? First, I realized that John had probably written this chapter against the background of an already existing sacramental practice. Reliable tradition suggests that John was the last Gospel to be written, the reason it is always listed as fourth. It was probably written to a church that had been engaged in eucharistic practice for some decades. The witness of Ignatius of Antioch and the *Didache* points to the Eucharist as a central part of the Church's worship by the end of the first century. So, when the early Christians read John chapter six, they would naturally have linked their practice to Jesus' words about eating His flesh and drinking His Blood just as they would have connected His words about being born of water and the Spirit in John chapter three to Baptism. I concluded that the early Church would have read this chapter sacramentally.

Second, Reformed Christians had taken the chapter quite literally when they cited John 6:44 to buttress their doctrine of unconditional election and 6:39 to support perseverance or even irresistible grace. If they were willing to take these texts as unmistakable evidence to support their doctrines, why would they not take 6:53-54 as unmistakable evidence that the Christian eats and drinks of Christ? I saw no reason to downplay the full impact of Jesus' words about eating His flesh and drinking His Blood. Third, all the Church Fathers confirmed that the early Church had linked John chapter six to the Eucharist as they also linked chapter three to Baptism. It was the Catholic interpretation that was standing in continuity with the early Church.

In my study, preparing to teach my students, I came to the conclusion that the Catholic view had a more coherent reading of John chapter six than the Reformed view. Anything less than a sacramental reading meant that Jesus' strong words were reduced only to acts of faith. Jesus' insistence on eating His flesh and drinking His Blood became, on the Reformed reading, a *mere metaphor*. But metaphors have a point to them, a reference beyond themselves; they generally point to something deeper, more profound. Was that faith? The Catholic way of reading the text saw faith in Christ as leading to the partaking of His flesh and Blood. I noticed a progression in John chapter six. The miracle of feeding the crowd naturally leads to faith in Jesus as the bread of life and faith in Him naturally leads to eating His flesh and drinking His Blood. The metaphor was not pointing to individual faith but to the reality that the Logos, the Son of Man, actually gives Himself fully, as God and man, to those who come to Him.

As I studied and reflected on the presence of Christ in the Eucharist, I decided that it would not be fair to study the Catholic teachings from a distance. It was time to leave the shallow waters of the Reformed shore to "put out into the deep" or, as the Latin of Luke 5:4 has it, *duc in altum*. I had to attend Mass, and it was in this experience that I realized that something greater had been there all along waiting for me to discover it.

CHAPTER FOUR

STARTLED BY A GREATER SACRAMENT
1992-1993

At noon, one day near the end of that fall semester in 1990, I walked for the first time through the large entryway into St. Peter's Catholic Cathedral in Jackson, Mississippi. The beauty of the sanctuary of this gothic church was astounding — the white marble altars, the brilliantly colored leaded-glass windows of biblical scenes, and the magnificent Venetian glass mosaic. At first, the language, gestures, and movements seemed foreign and strange. Not to be put off, however, I bought a Missal and searched our seminary library for commentaries on the Eucharistic Prayers. In time, I began attending Mass at the Cathedral more frequently. My wife and I would sometimes go to the vigil Mass at a church across town, while still attending our Presbyterian worship on Sunday morning, but I attended midday Mass whenever I could. After some time, I began to realize that my interest was so much more than intellectual curiosity. My heart was being won over by the beauty of the Mass. As I felt myself being drawn into the liturgy, I began to be afraid. Surely, I thought, I could not become a Catholic.

That year taught me something about myself which has been in my consciousness ever since. The delight that I found in prayer in the Catholic Cathedral in Jackson was like nothing I had ever known before. I began thinking of it as my prayer cave. I would dip down into the pew before Mass started and pour out my heart to God, begging Him to help me. The help I sought most was not so much about whether to become Catholic but to liberate me from my sinful tendencies. I was in need of profound moral reform. On the outside, everyone thought of me as a good upstanding Christian man; on the inside, there was anger, pride, and moral laxity. I needed true conversion and I begged God for it at every Mass.

The contrast between Mass on weekdays and Presbyterian worship on Sundays was striking. I had grown bored with my Presbyterian services, both as participant and as minister. Some Sundays I just couldn't wait for church to be over. Weekday Mass, however, even with no music, engaged my every sense and drew me into something larger and more wonderful than myself. It was as if the Mass was my secret hiding place where I met my beloved, Jesus, and reveled in His grace. There I had a growing sense of the real presence of Jesus in the world today.

A POINT OF NO RETURN

Sometime in the 1992-1993 academic year I reached a point of no return. The more daily Masses I attended and the more I learned of a Catholic way of praying, the clearer the path was becoming. The Mass was like a giant magnet pulling me into its grip. I simply loved the liturgy. I yearned to become a Catholic and if I had had a profession that did not involve the Presbyterian church directly, I am sure that I would have become a Catholic earlier. Yet, the more I considered my professional situation, the more I was torn up inside. It seemed foolhardy, even self-destructive, to become a Catholic.

One day I called a dear friend whom I could trust. After listening patiently to my dilemma, he asked, "Ken, do you want my honest opinion?" I assured him I did. "Ken, you'd be a fool to give up everything you have worked for in your life. You're not just an ordinary minister. You got a Ph.D. with the purpose in mind of teaching others who want to become ministers. Has your teaching been successful? From all I've heard you are a valued teacher at the seminary. Why do you want to throw that all away for some theological fancy?"

His words burned in my soul with a fire like purgatory (if there was such a place). Yet, somehow I couldn't shake the deep yearning I had for the sacraments, for prayer, and for the theological coherence of Catholicism. What was I going to do? Was I self-deceived?

God gave me the presence of mind, not to know the answer immediately, but to know where the answer could be found. Even though I had always professed with my lips the primacy of prayer, my actual practice had been to consult with others first and then to pray. Now I had to reverse that practice. So, I prayed at every Mass for God to reveal what He wanted me to do with my life. I knew instinctively that the Mass contained the answer somehow. So, I began to lay my request on the altar at every Mass.

At one weekday Mass, I entered St. Peter's Cathedral as I had done on most days for well over a year. That day the Mass was the same as I had come to love it. What had seemed foreign and strange was now precious and inviting, as if a gigantic tractor beam was drawing me into something greater than myself. When we came to the Communion Rite, the priest held up the host for all to see and said these words: "Behold, the Lamb of God who takes away the sins of the world. Happy are those who are called to his supper!" How many times I had seen this host before! And how many times I had believed those words with my mind! Today was somehow different. As I looked at the host in the hands of the priest, the words welled up from my soul, "I really believe that. This is truly the Son of God, the Lamb of sacrifice who takes away my sins." With a new and deeper meaning I said along with the congregation, "Lord I am not worthy to receive you but only say the word and I shall be healed." As I left St. Peter's Cathedral that day, I knew deep in my heart that someday I had to become Catholic. There was no turning back. This extraordinary experience came back to my mind years later when I was translating a homily by St. John Chrysostom (A.D. 347-407). This great preacher used a startling term to entice his hearers to the eucharistic table. In his homily entitled *On Blessed Philogonus*, preached five days before Christmas, Chrysostom called the Eucharist a *philtron*, a "love charm." He said, "Rather because of this I greet and love this day [of Christ's birth] and I put love front and center that I may make you sharers of this love charm." Later Chrysostom identified the manger of Bethlehem with the table of the Eucharist: "For when we approach with faith we too will certainly see him lying in the manger for this table fulfills the purpose of the manger." For me, the Eucharist passed from an external rite to a love charm that drew me into God's embrace.

By the summer of 1992, Sharon and I had had many conversations about the Catholic Church and its teachings. One such teaching that puzzled us both was on sexuality. We had always been opposed to abortion but did not see anything wrong with contraception. As I read and discussed these matters with Sharon, we became convinced that Pope Paul VI was right about the contraceptive mentality that had developed in America stemming from the sexual revolution of the 1960s. In 1982, when our third child was born, we had consented to have Sharon's fallopian tubes tied. Sharon is one of the most maternal women I have ever known and she grieved this loss quietly as I ignored her pain.

Newly influenced by natural moral law, we came to the conviction that we had made a great mistake. I began to grieve this loss as well and to believe that we had to do everything humanly possible to reverse the tubal ligation. Sharon was relieved and hopeful. That summer, Sharon and I traveled to Indiana where she underwent the procedure. Since this was not covered by insurance, we had to put out a large amount of our own money but we were determined to have more children if God so blessed us. In the months that followed we tried very hard to have more children believing in the words of Psalm 127 that "children are an inheritance of the Lord." But it was not to be.

SEEING CATHOLIC FAITH IN THE FLESH

During that same year a Catholic businessman had been calling me regularly to discuss various issues and to help me resolve them so that I might become a Catholic. He was persistent but I never felt repelled by him. One day he offered to pay my way to a summer conference where there would be several prominent Catholic speakers. When I arrived on the campus of Franciscan University in Steubenville (Ohio), I did not know what to expect. I certainly did not expect to find exuberant praise flowing from the mouths of Catholic Christians. I came to find out that this university was the center of a Catholic charismatic renewal of which I was totally ignorant.

I had been involved in various Protestant charismatic groups off and on in the 1970s but was always uncomfortable with their lack of theological and psychological stability. By the early 1980s, I no longer wanted to be in any charismatic group. However, there was something different about this Catholic charismatic experience at Steubenville. They had the same kind of "praise" music as other groups, complete with raised hands, clapping, and joyful singing, but this rather free-flowing worship was combined with a solemn and dignified celebration of the Mass.

The speakers at the conference were anything but the shallow and manipulative kind I had seen in Protestant charismatic circles. I don't recall much of the specifics of that weekend but I do remember being spellbound by the enthusiastic preaching of Fr. Michael Scanlan and Dr. Scott Hahn. I had become aware of Scott as a Presbyterian minister who had converted to the Catholic Church, a great encouragement for me to stay on the path. He and his wife, Kimberly, were gracious and welcoming people. Kimberly's father was Dr. Jerry Kirk, well-known in Presbyterian circles for his courageous fight against pornography in the Cincinnati area. Like her father, Kimberly was faith-filled. The other speakers too exhibited an attractive balance between vibrant faith and intellectual integrity. Professors Peter Kreeft and Thomas Howard were evidence enough that intellectually honest men could become Catholic with full integrity.

Two people in particular stood out and became lifelong friends. The first was Marcus Grodi, himself a Presbyterian minister, who was on the cusp of conversion. From the first time that I saw Marcus' pastoral face and heard his caring voice, I knew I had met a brother in Christ. After our meeting in Steubenville, Marcus regularly called me to offer encouragement and support.

The other was Marie Jutras, a woman about the age of my mother who had come down from Toronto with a group of fellow Canadians. As I sat talking to a man in the cafeteria one day during the conference, I mentioned the name of Bernard Lonergan whose books I had been reading. The man with whom I spoke had never heard of him. The woman sitting next me said quietly, "You know, Fr. Lonergan was a Canadian." "No, I didn't know that," I replied. Marie Jutras then went on to explain some of Fr. Lonergan's ideas in a way that left me spellbound. I thought to myself, "How does this Catholic laywoman know so much about theology?" I came to find out that Marie had studied theology and was very conversant in the Catholic Faith. More importantly, Marie showed me an openness and kindness that dispelled any doubts about the goodness of ordinary Catholic people.

That weekend showed me that there were perhaps many lay Catholics who were conversant with their faith on a deep level. It was just what I needed to see at that point in my life. Over the next two years, Marie would call our home at least once a month, not to push or prod, but to offer her support for my journey.

PRAYER IN A NEW VEIN

I discovered the rich writings of many Catholic saints during my two last years at Reformed Seminary. My work on Galileo had brought me into contact with the intellectual patrimony of the Jesuits but I also desired to explore the Ignatian heritage of the thirty-day retreat. An Irish missionary priest I knew recommended the writings of the founder of the Society of Jesus, St. Ignatius of Loyola. I bought André Ravier's *Do-It-At-Home Retreat* and Joseph Tetlow's *Ignatius Loyola: Spiritual Exercises*. Both books struck a responsive chord within me.

In the summer of 1993, I was ready to go on an Ignatian retreat, but, being a married man with many responsibilities, I could not go off by myself for thirty days. Ravier's book proved to be the answer. Here was a planned retreat that I could do by myself. Since Sharon was now fully aware of my journey, she agreed to do the retreat with me. The main motivation was spiritual, to know Jesus better; the Ignatian retreat seemed like a perfect answer.

The fundamental idea behind the Ignatian retreat is to meditate on the life of Jesus with the prayer that He would reveal His will. More than anything else, I wanted to know what He wanted me to do. As the retreat progressed, I came to the third week, which involves meditation on the passion and death of Jesus. This week held unexpected surprises but the truths I came to know were not without precedents in my life. When I was a young man, my heart had been captured by the story of Jesus in the garden of Gethsemane. Jesus' agony in seeking to do God's will, His offering of His life to the Father, and His willingness to endure suffering had made a lasting impression on me. I found myself longing to be like Jesus in the garden. The words of Fr. Joseph Tetlow in *Ignatius Loyola: Spiritual Exercises* guided my prayer:

> You will seriously pray the Passion only out of love
> for Jesus … In this week, you will hear Jesus call
> you no longer servant but friend. You are still a
> sinner, but what was a burden of your individual
> guilt and shame has become, by a kind of divine
> trick, a load of grief and pain that you are sharing
> with your Redeemer (p. 130).

I longed to love Jesus more. Though I was bearing my guilt and shame, I somehow felt them transformed into an opportunity to be healed and to become a healing for others. Then Fr. Tetlow characterized my experience perfectly:

> Directors know that people go through the Third
> Week in various ways according to many variables
> of temperament and experience. You may find
> yourself dry and stiff, like a sponge in a desert; per-
> haps God is leading you to share Jesus' desperate
> desolation. Or again, you may find yourself weep-
> ing much of the time; your hours may seem like an
> instant and the days, very short (p. 131).

As I meditated on Jesus in Gethsemane, I began to weep and could not contain my emotions. These were not superficial feelings; these were the deep experience of prayer and identification with Jesus that I had longed for my whole life but which had been unavailable to me in my Protestant experience. Then I read something that both comforted and frightened me:

One thing is sure: You will not decide how you are going to take part in Jesus' Passion. God's Spirit decides. In this, at least, you know His genuine powerlessness (p. 131).

These words were seared into my soul. I recalled Paul's words in 2 Corinthians 4:10, "We always carry around in our body the dying of Jesus that the life of Jesus may also be revealed in our body." I meditated a long time on these words as I saw Jesus in Gethsemane in my mind. I knew that not only had Jesus once suffered on the cross but that He also wanted to share His suffering with me. He wanted me to enter into His passion and to carry around, not His past death, but His current dying. I wrote in my journal:

> Lord, I am a little over forty years of age and have never known any real suffering. But I have now come to see that to be a true disciple, I must be willing to enter into Your sufferings if I am to be your agent of salvation for others. Lord, let me share Your sufferings.

As Fr. Tetlow had said, I had no idea how I would share in Jesus' passion. I only knew I was ready to do so. That willingness was both comforting and dangerous. In time, the Spirit of God would reveal how I would suffer with and for Jesus.

That experience of Ignatian prayer was so satisfying that I longed to drink from the wells of Catholic spirituality. My subsequent reading, meditation, and assimilation of great Catholic spiritual sources have proven my original instincts sound. There is nothing comparable in the Protestant world.

During the last year of my teaching at Reformed, I don't recall ever attending daily services in the seminary chapel but I took every opportunity to attend daily Mass. Unable to receive the Eucharist, I still sensed that the spiritual realities it embodied were already at work in my soul.

CHAPTER FIVE

A Year of Great Decisions
1993-1994

When the school year began in the fall of 1993, I hoped that someday I would become a Catholic. There were still many obstacles, most especially within my own soul. The more deeply I read the Church Fathers, the more thoroughly I understood the history of Christian worship (liturgy), and the more convinced I became of the distance between the faith of the Reformation and that of the ancient Church. The Episcopal Cathedral in Jackson, Mississippi is only a block away from the Catholic Cathedral. On special feast days, especially Holy Week, we attended the Episcopal Cathedral as a family. I even had a conversation with the president of our seminary in which I asked him if I could become an Episcopalian (Anglican) without relinquishing my position at the seminary. He quietly assured me that such a move was possible. As long as I was an Evangelical Anglican like James I. Packer or Alister McGrath, I was acceptable to the seminary. During my last academic year at the seminary (1993-1994), I began conversations with an Anglican priest who tried to persuade me to join. A few students who were inclined toward high church liturgy would join me every Friday at this priest's celebrations of the liturgy. I was on the road for sure but I was far from sure where it would end.

One day I picked up John Henry Newman's *Essay on the Development of Doctrine* written originally in 1844 as Newman was on the cusp of entering the Catholic Church. I could not put the book down. I would fall asleep at night reading it because it seemed to embody all my struggles. I remember one day in my office thinking, "This man walked the path I am now treading one hundred and fifty years before me." Within days I was in the seminary library checking out everything I could on Newman and the Oxford Movement, of which he was the leading light. As I read, I secretly hoped that my emerging faith and theology could be acceptable within the confines of the Reformed Faith and, therefore, save me from having to become Catholic! If I could do what the Oxford Movement did — have an ancient catholic faith within the structures of Protestantism — all would be well. Maybe I could retain my position at the seminary. It quickly became evident, however, that the Anglo-Catholicism of the Oxford Movement would not be acceptable within Presbyterianism.

Newman's theory of doctrinal development has been subject to much disagreement within Anglicanism and Catholicism but from the *Essay on the Development of Doctrine* I gleaned several important markers showing the way forward. The most important was his often quoted statement "To be deep in history is to cease to be Protestant." I came to the conviction that to be deep in history was to cease to be Reformed, but was all Protestantism out of the picture? It was Newman's *Tract 90* that convinced me of the truth of his statement. Newman published this tract, the last of the Tractarian or Oxford Movement, as an attempt to give *The Articles of Religion of the Anglican Church* (Thirty Nine Articles) a Catholic interpretation. He argued that the Thirty Nine Articles were not directed against the Council of Trent's dogmas but against a distortion of them. His implication was clear, that even Roman Catholic dogmas were within the boundaries of acceptable doctrine and therefore acceptable within the Church of England. The reaction to this publication was swift and scathing. Newman's own bishop condemned it. Countless others did as well.

I went back to the Thirty Nine Articles and reread them carefully. I concluded that Newman was involved in special pleading in *Tract 90*. I simply could not see how the pronouncements of the Council of Trent could be reconciled with the Thirty Nine Articles. This made clear to me that one had to choose between not only Calvinism and the Council of Trent but between Anglicanism and Roman Catholicism. Newman himself had come to the same conclusion and realized that he had to go to Rome. However, recognizing in one's head what one should do is not enough to compel sluggards. I needed a greater impetus.

I had to do something but I wasn't sure exactly what. The problems facing me were twofold, theological and practical. Theologically, there were still two doctrinal issues that I had not resolved, both of which would have decisive consequences. I had not resolved the central question of the Reformation — justification by faith alone — and I still was not sure about the role of the papacy in Christian unity. The first question concerning justification would determine whether I could remain a Protestant of any kind, and the second question about the divine authorization for the Petrine ministry would determine whether I would become Catholic or Orthodox. The practical problem, however, loomed even larger: if I left the seminary, how would I support my family?

In the fall of 1993, the president of the seminary invited me into his office for a chat. He told me that the seminary community was disturbed by rumors of my Catholic leanings. He was kind and even sympathetic, but he let me know that I was the only one who could dispel these rumors. He was a kind southern gentleman, who wanted the best for me, but he stressed that, if I didn't actively squelch these rumors, life for me at Reformed Seminary was not going to be smooth. He had no intentions of persecuting me or of hurting my career.

Yet, he and I both knew that I could not last long in a community where I was being perceived as a Catholic. This spurred me on to deal with the remaining issues.

THE QUESTION OF JUSTIFICATION BY FAITH

I now had to face the all pressing question of justification by faith alone. I had been putting off this issue because the answer I chose would be a real turning point for me. Martin Luther had said that this doctrine was the one on which the church stands or falls. If the church got this doctrine wrong, nothing else could be right. The purity of the gospel of Jesus Christ was at stake. I was torn up inside, pulled in two directions and ruled by fear. I feared that if I could not justify the Catholic doctrine of justification in my mind, I would be forced to remain a Presbyterian, but my heart was already persuaded for other reasons that I had to leave the Reformed Faith. On the other hand, I feared that if I found the Catholic doctrine of justification in accord with the Bible, I would have to leave everything I had known and loved.

Only God's grace gave me the will power to face the question of justification by faith alone. First, I reviewed the history behind the doctrine. The protest of the sixteenth century that became known as the Reformation was a complex historical movement with many facets but, from the point of view of doctrine, one of Martin Luther's most famous declarations stands out above all: that sinners are justified by faith alone as they trust in Jesus Christ. As a Presbyterian minister, I preached many sermons in which I gloried in the righteousness of Christ as our only hope of salvation.

To grasp properly the differences between the Catholic and Reformed views of this doctrine, I went back to make sure I understood the Reformed doctrine properly. After a thorough review of the Reformed creeds, I was convinced I had understood it properly. For a knowledgeable Presbyterian, salvation can only come through Christ alone (*solus Christus*) by the grace of God alone (*sola gratia*) and only through the instrumentality of faith (*sola fide*). This excluded the idea of any help from human resources, be they the living or the dead (saints). It excluded any work on our part. Works are important in the Reformed Faith but they play no role in our justification. It is God's favor alone upon our souls that saves (*sola gratia*). And most important of all, it must be only by faith because we believed that to add anything else to faith would cause our salvation to revert back to human effort. Reformed Christians loathed the idea that human power could save us. Trusting in human effort was the pernicious error of Romanism. Rome compromised God's grace by making works a part of salvation.

Understanding the Catholic view was more difficult and time consuming but the true differences between the Reformation and Catholic view became clear through patient and deliberate study. The Catholic view of justification is rooted, like everything else in Catholicism, in the reality of the Incarnation. When the Holy Spirit came upon the Virgin Mary in her womb and brought the Eternal Logos to her, God became flesh (Jn 1:14). The purpose of the Incarnation was to unite divinity with humanity forever. As St. Athanasius would put it, "the Son of God became the Son of Man that the sons of men might become the sons of God" (cf. St. Athanasius, *On the Incarnation*; also *Catechism of the Catholic Church*, paragraph 460). Interestingly, C.S. Lewis made a similar statement in *Mere Christianity*, restating St. Athanasius before him, "The Son of God became a man to enable men to become sons of God" (New York, Harper Collins edition, 2001; pg. 178). The Eastern Church Fathers called this process *theosis*, or the process of being infused with the Divine. Both Protestants and Catholics believe that Jesus Christ is, after the Incarnation, forever the God-Man but it is only in Catholicism that the Incarnation fits into the plan of salvation in the fullest way.

The Reformation doctrine of justification does not include, or at least does not emphasize, the union of human beings with God. Its doctrine is one of imputation, a legal declaration in which human beings are declared righteous before God's presence. In this view, it would have been sufficient for the Eternal Logos to become man, to suffer, to die on the cross, and to rise from the dead so that the merits of His death could be imputed to the sinner's account. There does not seem to be any further need for Christ to remain a man in heaven. He could have simply shed His humanity and returned to heaven in His divinity. In fact, I recall hearing Protestant Christians say occasionally that Jesus was no longer a man in heaven. I don't think their belief was just a matter of bad catechesis. Their system of thinking doesn't seem to require His continuing humanity.

The Catholic view of justification is infusion, a process in which God fills the human soul with His presence and therefore with His mercy, grace, and power. The permanence of the Incarnation makes more sense because the goal of God's redemptive plan is not just imputation but the uniting of Himself with human beings forever. A union took place first in Jesus Christ and it is that union which He shares with sinners so they can grow into human fullness by being made increasingly divine. This is essentially what the Apostle Peter meant when he said, "His divine power has granted to us all things that pertain to life and godliness, through the knowledge of him who called us to his own glory and excellence, by which he has granted to us his precious and very great promises, that through these you may escape from the corruption that is in the world because of passion, and become partakers of the divine nature" (2 Pet 1:3,4). In this view, the sacraments acquire a more direct relation to salvation. Beginning with Baptism, the sacraments infuse God's grace into the human soul and make it conformed to the image of Christ. Christ's merits are not accounted to the sinner but poured into the soul of the sinner.

Infusion implies a process, not a one-time act. In the Reformed creeds, justification is defined as an *act* of God's grace since it is an imputation of righteousness. In the Catholic view, God's grace is gradually poured into the soul of the believing Christian. The *Angelus*, a standard Catholic prayer, expresses it thus: "Pour forth, we beseech you, O Lord, your grace into our hearts that we, to whom the Incarnation of Christ your Son was made known by the message of an angel, may through his passion and cross, be brought to the glory of his resurrection." Salvation, therefore, is a process of growing in God's grace over a lifetime. One can be more or less justified. In Protestantism, however, one is either justified or not justified. In Reformed theology, sanctification is a process of growing in holiness but that process does not affect the state of one's justification. In Catholic theology, justification and sanctification are two biblical words describing the same process.

The process of sanctification or justification is, in the Catholic view, one of constant purgation, illumination, and union. Purgation is the removal of sin and the inclinations to sin known as concupiscence. As the Christian receives more and more grace, he grows less inclined to sin and more inclined to obey God. This was why John wrote his first Epistle: "My little children, I am writing this to you so that you may not sin" (1 Jn 2:1a). If this purgative process is not complete at death, there remains a final purgation after death for those who die in a state of grace and, thereby, are destined for heaven. The removal of sin and the accompanying propensities to sin are not enough; a person on the spiritual journey needs illumination, an infusion of the knowledge of God. As a person becomes holier through purgation, their vision of God, the world, and themselves becomes clearer through illumination. Paul used such language in praying for the Ephesians, namely, "that the eyes of their hearts might be enlightened" (Eph 1:18; see also Col 1:9-11). The final end of this process is complete union with God described by the medieval theologians as the Beatific Vision. It is what Jesus spoke of when He said, "Blessed are the pure in heart for they will see God" (Mt 5:8). Purgatory, and the process of growing in holiness through purgation, make perfect sense on the Catholic view but absolutely no sense on the Protestant view.

En route to the Beatific Vision, the ordinary Christian engages in works of grace, that is, works motivated by grace. Here is where Protestants are likely to misunderstand the Catholic view. In Reformed Protestantism, works are evidence of genuine faith. They are necessary because without works one cannot know whether one is saved. Works are motivated by grace but they do not contribute to one's justification since God has already completed that act. Works only show us whether that act has occurred or not. In the Catholic view, good works are motivated by grace and open up our hearts to receive more grace being poured into our souls. Grace does not come from us; it comes from the merits of Christ. Christ alone can merit heaven and our final union with God, but He must communicate those merits for us to have any hope of the Beatific Vision. Good works are the ongoing means of Christ communicating His merits; works can include prayer, obedience, sacrifice, sufferings, and acts of charity. They help us cooperate with God by expanding our hearts to receive more of God.

The importance of the Eucharist to the Catholic view of justification then became clear. If justification was a process of becoming more and more just through the infusion of grace, there had to be a means by which that grace was continually infused into our souls. The answer lay in the sacraments and preeminently in the greatest of the sacraments, the Eucharist. All the sacraments give grace but only the Eucharist gives the Author of grace. The Eucharist gives grace not only in a generic sense; it gives Christ Himself in the fullness of His humanity and divinity. As is often said in Catholic life, it gives the Body, Blood, Soul, and Divinity of Christ. Here too was the reason for Jesus being forever the God-Man. In the Incarnation, divinity was united with humanity in the Person of Jesus Christ. The union of divinity and humanity is communicated to the Christian through the holy Eucharist. And the faithful Catholic can be reminded of this truth every Mass in the words spoken by the priest (or deacon) as he mixes the water and wine, "By the mystery of this water and wine may we come to share in the divinity of Christ, who humbled himself to share in our humanity."

The fundamental mistake of justification by faith alone is that it transfers the once-for-all-ness of Jesus' death — the objective part of redemption — to God's act of forgiveness in response to our faith, the subjective part of redemption. If you believe that all sins — past, present, and future — are forgiven in one act of declaration made by God at the moment of faith, then there is little reason to ask for forgiveness in the future. Why ask forgiveness for sins already forgiven? Yet Reformed Christians do ask forgiveness for their daily sins. Something is wrong in either their theory or their practice. I concluded that their practice was right but their theory was wrong.

In the end, I came to believe that the Protestant view of salvation was insufficient, lacking the fullness of the Christian Faith. While not everything in the Protestant view needed to be rejected, the Catholic view represented better the teaching of the whole New Testament. If the Catholic view had been what most Protestants thought it was — salvation by works or faith plus works — I would have rejected it and still be a Protestant today. The Catholic view, however, is truer to the New Testament and agrees with the Church Fathers better than the imputation view. The Catholic view had fifteen hundred years of theological support behind it. The Protestant view was a kind of innovation out of accord with the way Christians in earlier centuries had understood salvation.

Though I did not see it at the time, I came later to observe that this doctrine of salvation and heaven makes some practical differences in the lives of faithful Catholics. I never saw in the Protestant Christians the yearning for holiness I have observed in some Catholics. I myself didn't have yearnings to such a degree nor do I think I saw it in others. I have seen a life of prayer and holiness in some Catholics that borders on the phenomenal. I now think I know why. If you view yourself as already saved, as most Protestant Evangelicals do, then there may be less reason to pursue a life of prayer and holiness. Of course, many Evangelicals are holy but there is also a level of holiness in Catholics that I never had an inkling of as a Protestant. Since Catholics view their salvation as an ongoing project of conversion, consisting of justification and sanctification, they are motivated to pursue holiness to a much greater degree.

My renewed study of justification left me with one clear decision: I could not in good conscience remain a Protestant of any kind. As a result, I could not remain at Reformed Seminary. I had to become either Catholic or Orthodox, a decision that would depend on my study of the Petrine office. As I moved closer to the ancient Christian Faith with every theological decision, I knew something greater was waiting for me.

✠

CHAPTER SIX

ROME OR ORTHODOXY?

1994

In God's providence, I had a sabbatical coming up in the fall of 1994. Reformed Seminary normally granted one semester off from teaching to allow a professor to write. Earlier, I had made a request for two semesters but it was denied. I had been accepted as a Ph.D. candidate at Lancaster University in the United Kingdom, under Dr. John Hedley Brooke. Dr. Brooke was a former Editor of the *British Journal for the History of Science*, and was then on the faculty of Lancaster as a Professor of the History of Science. I was bringing all of my studies on Copernicanism and Galileo together into a dissertation on the interpretation of Scripture and astronomy.

By this time, however, Catholicism was oozing out of me. Everyone could see it. So when the Dean of the Faculty offered me two semesters of a sabbatical if I promised not to return to the seminary at the end of that year, I jumped at the chance. Now I had the prospect of a whole year's salary so I could finish my second dissertation while looking for a new position. Our family made plans to move back to Bloomington, the place most familiar to our children.

As my son and I packed the U-Haul truck in the summer of 1994, a deep sense of loss engulfed me. Yes, I had to leave Reformed Seminary but the reason was my own choice. They had sufficiently warned me that only I could stop the rumors about my Catholic sympathies. No one had been nasty or belligerent. They simply wanted me gone. I had become a liability. The leaders of Reformed Seminary were ambivalent. They had said many times that I was one of their best teachers. The chairman of the board had reached out to me in a special way. The president was always a perfect gentleman. My older colleagues in the Biblical Studies division of the seminary continued to lavish love and friendship on us. It was painful to leave behind people and a school into which I had poured seven years of my life. Something important to me was slipping away. Yet, strange as it might seem, I was at peace. That sense of loss was accompanied by a sense of gain, not of what I had at the moment, but of what lay in front of me. I was hoping for a better future for my family and for a different academic position. Most of all, I hoped to gain entrance into what I had come to believe was the true Church of Jesus Christ and to receive the holy Eucharist.

As we got settled into our new home in Bloomington, the children became involved in school and wholesome activities. The History and Philosophy of Science Department at Indiana University welcomed me within its confines as I was writing the final chapters of my dissertation. They appointed me a Visiting Professor and gave me one class to teach on the history of science and religion while one retired professor graciously allowed me to share his office. I became a regular member of their intellectual community.

Our family had to decide where we would attend church. The many conversations that Sharon and I had already had about the Eucharist had shown her that the sacramental views of the Reformed (Presbyterian) faith were deficient. My professional studies had taken me deeply into the waters of Lutheran theology, and it was clear that their creeds contained a belief in the real presence of Christ in the sacrament of the altar. The fact that they professed the real presence, however, did not mean that they actually possessed it, but at least they believed in the importance of the Lord's Supper in a manner superior to the Reformed Faith.

Consequently, we decided that we would attend a Lutheran Church of the Missouri Synod, which was still faithful to their creeds of the sixteenth century. We made many new friends, and our oldest daughter Rebekah and I became members of the choir. I, however, continued attending daily Mass at one of the three Catholic churches in Bloomington, and was becoming known to the Catholic community.

Some of the Lutherans learned that I had been a Presbyterian minister and suggested that I become an ordained Lutheran pastor. If friendship and personal comfort were the deciding factors, I would have gladly done so. However, I had already concluded that the Lutheran doctrine of justification was not biblically or historically faithful. I had also concluded that to have a valid Eucharist, one must have a valid priesthood and I could not see that the Lutherans had it. There were only two candidates: the Roman Catholic Church or one of the Orthodox churches. These were the only ones that possessed valid priestly ordination. The deciding factor, theologically speaking, would be the role of Peter in the leadership of Christ's Church.

THE FINAL ISSUE: ROME OR ORTHODOXY?

Sometimes it is easier to leave where one has been than to know where one is going. In my case, the ultimate decision was being prolonged because I had long been convinced that whatever decision I made needed to be permanent. I wasn't going to join just any church. I wanted to find the true, historic Church of Jesus Christ. Repeatedly, I prayed Psalm 86:11, "Teach me your way that I may walk in your truth. Unite my heart to revere your name." I prayed for the grace to be open to truth, to be able to see the path clearly, even if it should lead me away from the Catholic Church.

When I left Reformed Seminary I had concluded that I needed to be in a church that possessed true apostolic succession.

My seminary professor in the 1970s had declared that apostolic succession was a contradiction in terms. For him, as for many other Reformed people, the twelve Apostles were the unrepeatable foundation of the Church. Consequently, they denied that there was any apostolic authority associated with the office of bishop. Looked at from another vantage point, however, Reformed Protestants believed in a kind of apostolic succession, that of passing on the content of the faith in the New Testament.

For the Catholic Church, as for the Orthodox churches, the bishops of the early Church were the successors of the Apostles in that their authority carried the authority of the Apostles into succeeding generations. This is clear from writers as early as Clement of Rome in his *Letter to the Corinthians* (chapter 44), "Our apostles knew from our Lord Jesus Christ that there would be contention over the title of the bishop's office. For this reason, having received perfect foreknowledge, they appointed those mentioned before and afterwards gave the provision that, if they should fall asleep, other approved men would succeed their ministry." Having concluded from writers such as Clement and Irenaeus that the early Church did indeed believe in the passing on (*traditio*) of the apostolic office, I now only needed to decide which churches possessed that succession from the Apostles.

Why was this issue so important? It was because the validity of the Eucharist depended on it. I had become convinced that a valid Eucharist required a valid priesthood and the latter required apostolic succession. If I was to receive the true Eucharist from the hands of a priest, he, therefore, had to be truly ordained in a line of succession reaching back to the Apostles. It made sense that those churches which possessed such a succession were those who believed it was essential to the church and for the Eucharist, for, otherwise, why would a church insist on apostolic succession if it did not believe that such was necessary to be a valid church and have a valid sacrament? This left me with only two choices: either the Catholic Church united with the See of Peter or one of the Eastern Orthodox jurisdictions.

The question of Eastern Orthodoxy or Rome is a complicated one, which can be studied from many angles. I began with their broad agreement on some issues. They agreed on the four major Patriarchates in the ancient church (Jerusalem, Antioch, Alexandria, Rome) and then a fifth that became important after Constantine (Constantinople). They agreed that the Church of Rome and all the Eastern churches had a valid priesthood and a valid Eucharist. They believed in the decisive importance and continuing relevance of the historical creeds and ecumenical councils, at least the first seven councils. In some general sense, they affirmed the relevance of the Vincentian Canon of *ubique* (everywhere), *semper* (always) and *ab omnibus* (by all). They believed that there needed to be a visible expression of unity among all the churches. They agreed that Peter was the first Bishop of Rome and that the subsequent bishops of Rome were the successors of Peter. They agreed that the Bishop of Rome had a primacy in some sense.

The division between the East and Rome had to do with the precise role of Peter and his successors. The Eastern Orthodox affirmed a primacy of honor for the Bishop of Rome but denied a primacy of jurisdiction. The Catholic Church claimed that the Bishop of Rome was given a primacy of jurisdiction, not to rule over the other churches as a dictator, but to bring unity to Christendom. As I learned more of the Eastern Orthodox churches, I became troubled with the idea of autocephalous (self-governing) churches. The eastern churches are united by their common doctrine (i.e., by their adherence to the first seven ecumenical councils). Many of them (but not all) are united by a common liturgy such as the Liturgy of St. John Chrysostom. However, the governance of each autocephalous (or even national) church is largely independent of one another. Their leaders may seek to be unified in their decisions but there is little or no structural means for governmental unity.

The Church of Rome, or better, all the churches in communion with the Bishop of Rome are united by doctrine and structural governance. Even the eastern Catholic churches (e.g., Byzantine Rite Catholics), which have a distinct Canon Law, are united under the Bishop of Rome as the indisputable successor of Peter. What particularly struck me was how the office of Peter (Pope) appears differently inside the Church from the way it appears outside the Church. The Pope is not a kind of CEO of the Catholic Church, issuing dicta and pronouncements at whim. Reading St. John Paul II's teaching on the eastern churches, and his encyclical *Ut Unum Sint*, helped me to understand that the primary role of the Bishop of Rome was that of Unifier. The Pope was not some absolute monarch over the whole of Christendom but called to be a sign and instrument of holding the Church together in doctrine, in worship, and in witness to the unbelieving world. In other words, the Petrine office is a *structural means* of promoting unity.

Did Christ intend to establish a special office with Peter as its first holder? Did He give Peter a unique role among all the Apostles and, if so, what was that role? The answer had to be sought in the four New Testament passages that were most crucial to this issue: Matthew 16:13-20; 18:15-18; Luke 22:31-32; and John 21:15-19.

Matthew 16:13-20 was clear enough for me. Here Jesus gave the keys of the Kingdom to Peter alone. But Matthew 18:15-18 seemed to give the authority of binding and loosing to all the Apostles. While Matthew 16:19 uses the singular "you" (thou), Matthew 18:18 uses the plural "you." I came to this conclusion: while all the Apostles (and their successors) were given the authority "to bind and to loose," it was only in union with Peter, the sole holder of the Keys, that they could exercise that right. Peter was to act as "first among equals" (*primus inter pares*).

My interpretation of the Matthean texts best fit the passage in Luke 22:31-32. Here Jesus singles out Peter for a special role, "Simon, Simon! Satan has sought to sift you (pl) like wheat. But I have prayed for you (sg) that your (sg) faith not fail. And when you (sg) are turned around, strengthen your brothers." If Satan's desire was to destroy all the Apostles (you plural), why would Jesus only pray for Peter (you singular)? The answer is there for all to see. Peter will function as the encourager of his fellow Apostles. This is the exact role for Peter's successors, the bishops of Rome. The Roman bishop (or Pope) is there to strengthen his brothers: they must be united with him.

It made sense to me that Peter would again be singled out in John 21:15-19 after his threefold denial of Jesus. Jesus asks Peter three times if he loves the Lord. There are several striking facets to this passage but the most relevant is Jesus repeating His command to Peter, "Feed my sheep" (verses 15,16,17). Why would Peter be singled out for this command if all the Apostles were to be shepherds of the Church? I had to conclude that it was because Jesus intended Peter to be the shepherd of the shepherds under Himself as the Great Shepherd of the Sheep (Heb 13:20).

These passages in the New Testament all pointed in the same direction as ancient witnesses to the role of the Roman bishop. It was not that Rome per se was important. It was that Peter ended his life and ministry as the first Bishop of Rome. It was not simply that the pagan city of Rome was the preeminent city of the empire; it was that Peter was the preeminent leader of the Apostles.

As a result, I became humbly convinced that Christ intended to establish a Petrine office in the Church, and I had to be in union with that office. The school year 1994-1995 was a year of loss but I knew deep within my heart that there was something greater out there waiting for me. By Christmas of 1994, I had arrived at my final decision. While the Eastern Orthodox churches retained much of ancient Christianity, I had to enter the Roman Catholic Church because the Petrine office was the God-given structure to bring about and maintain unity.

SEVERING TIES WITH PRESBYTERIANISM

The time had come for me to deal with my Presbytery. Every Presbyterian minister is a member, not of his local church, but of the regional body known as a Presbytery, somewhat analogous to a diocese. Most ministers are members of the Presbytery in which they geographically reside and serve. Seminary professors, however, can serve outside the bounds of their Presbytery. I had become a member of the Warrior Presbytery in western Alabama. Now, in 1994, the chairman of the ministerial committee said that I needed to decide something. In light of my Catholic leanings, he suggested that I talk with a prominent Reformed theologian, Dr. James I. Packer. Perhaps he thought that if anyone could call me back from Rome, it would be Dr. Packer.

James I. Packer was an Evangelical Anglican theologian well respected in Reformed circles. He was a gentleman of the highest order. Dr. Packer had formulated the differences between Rome and the Reformation as residing in one's view of the work of the Holy Spirit. How one sees the work of the Spirit determines one's view of the church. He challenged me to show where the New Testament taught the sacramental system of the Catholic Church. The Calvinist view sees the first and primary object of the Spirit's ministry as the human heart. The Spirit must bring new life to dead souls through the preaching of the gospel, which leads to overwhelming emphasis on preaching in the Puritan tradition. This tradition has been preserved among traditional Presbyterians and low-church Anglicans like Packer. The worship of the church and the sacraments are important as aids in fostering this work of the Spirit in the individual heart. As people come together to form local churches, the word of God and sacraments are Christ's means of grace in fostering the Spirit's work.

Catholics will recognize much that is true and valuable in this view but will find a crucial difference of emphasis. In the Puritan view, the church is a result of the Spirit's work in the individual hearts of those who come together. His work in the sacrament is mediated by the individuals who come together to celebrate it. It is a bottom-up view. The Catholic view is a top-down view. My challenge was to explain how the sacramental view of Catholicism grew out of the New Testament. This proved easier than I had imagined. I explained how the Letter to the Hebrews taught that the high priesthood of Christ was a continuing ministry of our Lord in heaven, a point that no Evangelical would deny. Christ won for us eternal redemption by offering Himself *through the Eternal Spirit* (Heb 9:12-14). Christ took His temporal sacrifice into the eternal throne room of the Father and, by the ministry of the Holy Spirit, the sacrifice of His Body and Blood cleanses our consciences from dead works. Hebrews chapter twelve teaches that the Blood of Christ is now in heaven in the Body of Christ. Hebrews 12:24 teaches that the Church approaches the Blood of Christ in the divine liturgy. We who worship come "to the sprinkled blood that speaks better than the blood of Abel." The Blood of Christ speaks better than the blood of Abel because the latter cried out for vengeance while Christ's Blood cries out for mercy.

Christ's priesthood is at the *center of earthly Christian worship*. Indeed, that is what makes worship *Christian*. We are in heaven partaking of Christ's Blood and He is with us on earth. Hebrews 12:22-24 states that in the heavenly Jerusalem the Church approaches the myriads of angels and saints (i.e. "spirits of righteous men made perfect"). The essence of Catholic worship is the union of heaven and earth in the Divine Liturgy. Through worship (the Mass), we come to share in the Blood that speaks better than Abel's blood. Such worship is filled with the crucified and risen Lord. The Holy Spirit is the instrument for bringing the realities of Christ's redeeming death to earth, not by a re-crucifixion but by *anamnesis*, by making present the once-and-for-all sacrifice of Calvary. The Catholic Church sees the ministry of the Spirit as focused on the worship of the Church because this Spirit brings us the Lord Jesus in all His fullness. The New Testament supports this Catholic view of worship in its teaching on the priesthood of Christ and on how this priesthood is brought to us in the worship of the Body of Christ.

Dr. Packer graciously received my communications but our subsequent conversations brought us to a point of genuine division. He insisted that the New Testament did not authorize the sacramental system of Catholicism. My own wrestling with the Letter to the Hebrews had convinced me that the New Testament strongly supports the Catholic understanding of worship.

It was time for the Presbytery to act. The chairman of the ministerial committee and I agreed that we should proceed as painlessly and inconspicuously as possible. There was a provision in the *Book of Church Order* of the Presbyterian Church of America that allowed a minister to withdraw his credentials if he found himself out of accord with the Presbyterian creedal standards. I simply wrote a formal letter of withdrawal to my Presbytery and ceased functioning as a Presbyterian minister. Although it was a necessary move, it still brought a sense of loss for Sharon and for me.

CHAPTER SEVEN

✠

SHARING CHRIST'S SUFFERINGS

1995-1996

The prayer I had said in the summer of 1993, "Lord allow me to share more deeply in the sufferings of my Savior," seemed not to be answered. If it was being answered at all, it was only in small ways. I didn't feel that I was suffering.

After leaving Reformed Seminary, I still had a salary from my sabbatical year, but the prospects for a long term academic position seemed slight. In December of 1994, I received a notice that the history department at the University of Notre Dame was seeking a historian of science and religion. Given my present Ph.D. studies under Dr. Brooke, this job description seemed to have been written for me. Surely, I thought, only the special providence of God would bring this about. Many qualified applicants would apply but I still hoped to be chosen. My hopes heightened when I was granted a first interview. I was happy to envision service to the Church at Notre Dame. I don't know how the committee read me but I was certainly enthusiastic about Catholicism. However, my hopes were dashed when I was not invited to campus. The disappointment was so great because I had come so close. If ever there were a perfect fit, the Notre Dame job was it. But it was not to be. It was time to trust God for the future and to hope.

Soon, a friend, who was also interested in the relation of science to religion, approached me about a position at Redeemer College, a Reformed institution located in Ancaster, Ontario. Here too was an opportunity to support my family that seemed like the perfect fit. Jitse was a man of high integrity and so it was with a lump in my throat that I told him that I could not accept the position because I intended to become a Catholic. To my surprise, he said that being a Catholic did not necessarily preclude me from the position. However, the administration of the college disagreed. My hopes, once again, were dashed.

As 1994 passed into the winter of 1995, Sharon went to work outside the home as our family funds were becoming depleted by the expense of our daughter's illness. While still in Jackson, Mississippi, our oldest daughter had come down with a debilitating illness that had now grown worse. By Christmas of 1994, she had become close to death, or so we believed. Her long protracted illness was also having a visible effect on our son and youngest daughter. They were feeling cheated. So much time and attention were being directed to our oldest, where did they count in our family? Sharon and I too were in despair. One morning early in December, I sat at my computer in my office at the university with my hands trembling, unable even to type a message to a friend. I felt like giving up life. One that we had loved so dearly was on the verge of death. There is no suffering like that of a parent.

The spring of 1995 was a continuation of the desperation that Sharon and I felt over our daughter's illness and the general problems we were having with our children. We felt suffering through Lent but now it was the Easter season. Couldn't we experience the joy of the Lord, some glimmer of happiness that might encourage us? One day in almost total hopelessness I put my studies aside and read Psalm 86. This Psalm, overflowing with praise and thanksgiving to God, became a source of constant strength for me during this period. The Psalmist prays for our Lord to make glad the heart of His servant. I read this to Sharon and we both began to pray for the joy of the Lord to be our strength.

Easter Sunday of 1995, however, was anything but a day of joy. All Sharon and I could manage was to pull ourselves out of bed to attend Sunday morning services at the Lutheran church. Yet, as the Easter season progressed, we began to see some light at the end of the tunnel. Our daughter had begun to get the medical help she needed. I felt some satisfaction in my professional work in teaching and writing. On the latter score, I was making good progress on my second dissertation, expecting to finish it by mid-summer. I taught a class at Indiana University on science and religion in which I befriended a young man who later went on to become a Catholic theologian. He claims it was that class which saved his faith. All this was gratifying, but not much had changed in our external circumstances. All we could do was trust that ahead of us, by God's mercy, was a brighter day.

June 3, 1995 was a sunny afternoon, just the kind that made me happy to live in this quiet college town. Walking to my office, I was grateful for the previous evening when I celebrated with my family my forty-third birthday. Even though the year had been difficult emotionally, I sensed the goodness of God beneath it all.

As I rounded the corner of the building near my office, I quickened my step as I walked past a young man sitting on the sidewalk. I was in such a hurry that I didn't notice something odd: he was wearing a heavy coat on such a warm day. Having walked past him about ten feet, I was stunned by the loudest sound I have ever heard. Turning around to see what it was, I found myself looking down the barrel of a 9-millimeter semi-automatic held by a man in his twenties. Suddenly, as I heard him fire the gun again, I felt a stinging in my neck. Without any conscious thought, I turned and ran as fast as I could down the side of the building where he could not see me. Little did I know at the time that he moved to a position where he could see me and fired three more shots, all of them missing me. Once I was among the trees I felt my neck. When I took my hand away, I found it was full of blood. Only then did I realize that I had been shot.

I kept running until I met some people who helped me. As I sat on the stonewall next to the university chapel, I became hysterical and wondered why anyone would want to kill me. Providentially, a member of the Lutheran church was there who immediately called the pastor, Lawrence Mitchell.

Pastor Mitchell gathered my children from various places and brought them to the hospital as I lay in the emergency room waiting for the doctor. My voice was gone because the bullet had passed through the cartilage that held my vocal cords together. All I could do was hold up a written note to my wife and children around me, "I love you."

I don't remember the next four days as I was heavily sedated for the surgeries that hopefully would enable my vocal cords to heal, and allow me once again to have the blessed gift of speech. When I did awake, I found my parents sitting next to me, and I exclaimed in a painful, raspy, yet audible voice, "Mom, Dad, what are you doing here?" My parents had come up from Florida. Only later did I learn of the trial Sharon endured as she was detained by the police and, for a few short minutes, even suspected of being behind the shooting. I was shot in the very place where she was to pick me up. Sharon's father kept vigil outside my hospital room to protect me in case the perpetrator came back to finish the job. To this day, the shooter has never been identified.

The next three or four days were mixed with a sense of fear and a comforting sense of the presence of God. My wife never left my side. She brought me all my Catholic religious paraphernalia, such as a rosary, candles, and prayer books. Even though she could not use these things for her own spiritual nourishment, she knew how important they were to me. I had had many reasons to love Sharon in the past but never more than now.

The love of others was overwhelming. Friends from all over called to offer their support and encouragement: Catholics, Lutherans, Presbyterians, and Evangelicals all supported me. Catholics from a distance called to offer prayer and support. A Mass was to be offered for my healing at the Defending the Faith Conference the next week. All the priests I knew in Bloomington came to visit and one administered the Sacrament of Holy Anointing. Protestant pastors all came to visit, even the pastor of the Presbyterian church where I had been the founding pastor. Most memorable, though, was the diligent service of Rev. Mitchell, the Lutheran pastor. He came to see me every day in the hospital, to read Scripture, and to pray with my wife and me. My older brother called to encourage me to forgive the assailant in my heart. I mustn't let bitterness rule me. Lying in a hospital bed, I couldn't help believing that God was answering my prayer to share in the sufferings of Christ for the benefit of His people. I had long prayed for the greater visible unity among Christians. Now my sufferings were the occasion of Christians coming together for prayer and for service.

THE AFTERMATH OF THE SHOOTING

Sharon's whole family was wonderful. Her older brother David, a composer, wrote a special hymn for me that spoke of sharing Christ's sufferings. Her younger brother, who had been a policeman in Florida for many years, came up to support our family. He and my son found the bullets shot by the gunman. Sharon's sister had her children all pen notes of encouragement to me. Sharon's family proved to be truly Christian and supportive.

My children all reacted differently. Rebekah our eldest expressed great confidence in God's power to bring us through this horrible experience. Colin our son seemed bewildered but the presence of Sharon's younger brother from Florida seemed to help. I can vividly recall my son driving me to Mass the next Saturday, one week after the shooting. As we drove along the streets of the university en route to St. Charles' Church, I remember looking at the people walking calmly along the road. I thought, "Don't these people know they are in mortal danger?" My perspective on daily life had been radically altered. That evening at the Vigil Mass I couldn't hold back the tears. I was so thankful just to be alive and at the altar of God.

Still, though, I was not yet a Catholic.

For about a week my in-laws insisted that we stay at their home in case the gunman might return, since the local newspaper, for some inconceivable reason, had printed our address the day after the shooting. During this time at my in-laws, I had a conversation with Rachel our youngest in which she wondered about how I could trust God in the light of this tragedy. I assured her that there was nowhere else to turn. I hoped that she would learn the same trust over time.

Not long afterwards, my family in Florida invited us down for a vacation. My older brother provided an apartment for us. Later, my parents allowed Sharon and me to use their mountain cabin in North Carolina to spend a week in prayer together.

BACK TO NORMAL LIFE?

How does one return to life after such an event? I was like a wounded soldier coming home. Life would never be the same. Yet, eventually the same responsibilities and obligations returned.

Now I was no longer receiving any income from Reformed Seminary. Sharon and I worked odd jobs, piecing an income together as best we could. I couldn't imagine moving since it was Rebekah's last year of high school. I thought of starting a housing painting business to be called Contemplative House Painters.

I wondered if God was asking me to put the academic life behind me. Yet, in the fall of 1995, I traveled to Lancaster University in the United Kingdom to defend my second doctoral dissertation. On arrival at my meeting with the committee, I was told that my dissertation was so exceptional that they had already decided that I passed even before the verbal defense. They said it was an unusual decision but that the quality of the work was extraordinary. My advisor, Dr. Brooke, remarked that I had shown extraordinary perseverance in the face of overwhelming obstacles. All I could do was to thank God.

At that time, a Ph.D. plus a dollar would buy a nice cup of coffee in America. Some academic opportunities in the history of science were discussed among my colleagues but nothing concrete materialized. I was cut off from opportunities in my Protestant past because of my Catholic inclinations. Since I was not yet a Catholic, few Catholic institutions would look seriously at me. I didn't want to move my family again. Our financial needs were met partly through my wife's family. Sharon and I worked part-time for her brother David in his music business where I had worked during graduate school.

BECOMING A CATHOLIC FINALLY

In the spring of 1996 my older brother called from Florida. He asked me to pray about returning to Florida permanently to be around my parents and the family. I was the only child who had ever lived outside of Florida for any length of time. He thought it would be good for everyone. I told him that I did not have any job prospects in the Tampa area. My brother had been quite successful in real estate and offered me a job. The idea of entering the business world did not appeal to me but I told him I would pray about it.

It is not clear why I didn't move ahead with becoming a Catholic but I suppose I was waiting to see if my wife would join me. As I began asking God whether I should move back to Tampa, I noticed my thoughts moving in a positive direction. I told God that I was willing to do whatever He wanted me to do but that I needed Him to show me His will. I decided to go to the one place where I knew for sure that Jesus was.

Late one night, at the beginning of May, I went to St. Charles Borromeo Church to pray. They had a custom of keeping the church open twenty-four hours a day for people to pray when they felt the need. I certainly felt the need. I had come to cherish times of prayer before the Blessed Sacrament, believing that Jesus was present there in His divinity and His humanity.

As I knelt before the tabernacle, all alone in that beautiful church, I asked God to show me whether I should move back to Florida. "Lord, you know that I don't really want to go back but if you want me to, I will do your will." As if Jesus were speaking to me from the tabernacle, I heard, "Ken, the question is not what I want you to do. You want to do my will and I place my will in your heart for you to do it. What is it that you want to do most of all?" I responded, "Lord, I don't care if I never move back to Florida. I just want to become a Catholic." Then, as if with an inaudible whisper, Jesus seemed to say, "Well, then, what are you waiting on?" Now I knew that the time had come. No more waiting. Subsequent events bore this out. My brother withdrew his offer of a job, so Florida was no longer in the offing. But I knew that the most difficult conversation still lay ahead — a conversation with Sharon.

I told her that I believed I had to become a Catholic because I also believed that I would be sinning against God not to do so. I had long ago read the passage in *Lumen Gentium*, "Those who know the Catholic Church as founded by Christ as necessary and do not enter it, cannot be saved." I had become convinced that the Catholic Church was the true Church of Jesus Christ, and, therefore, I had to follow my conscience. Sharon told me that this was the very reason she could not become Catholic — her conscience. She was not convinced that the Catholic Church was the true Church and, therefore, could not enter it.

In our honest evaluations, we had reached a crossroads where we had never wanted to be. But by the mercy and grace of God, we stood face to face, hand in hand, with a love that only God can give. We have always believed that to the extent that a husband and wife each grow closer to Christ, they grow closer to each other, so we vowed together to support each other as we each followed our consciences. For now, trusting in God, we would be members of different churches, but we committed ourselves to family unity for the sake of our children. Sharon agreed to attend Mass with me at the Saturday Vigil, and I would attend the Lutheran church with her and the children on Sunday mornings.

The day of my confirmation was set for June 1, 1996. I called my Catholic friends who all affirmed that they would join me in prayer from a distance. Especially supportive were those two friends mentioned in chapter seven. Marcus Grodi and his Coming Home Network offered their fraternal love and support in an unprecedented way, while Marie Jutras, my Canadian mentor, promised to drive down from Toronto.

That June day, a year after I had almost been killed, I stood in the chapel of St. Charles Borromeo Church in Bloomington to profess that I believed everything that the holy Catholic Church teaches. Two other events made that day special. Our daughter Rebekah, who had been so seriously ill, graduated from high school. It was also my forty-fourth birthday. I couldn't help seeing the parallel between my experience and that of John Henry Newman who also entered the Catholic Church from Protestantism in his forty-fourth year. My life was nowhere as illustrious as his but that didn't matter. I was just happy to be home in the Catholic Church.

Since Conversion

1996-2015

S ince the day of my conversion to the Catholic Church I have
never doubted that it was the right decision. Though feelings of nostalgia and the loss of friends sometimes touch me,
I have been sure that the Catholic Church is my true spiritual
home. A year after my own confirmation, my oldest daughter
Rebekah, who was then in her first year of college, was also
confirmed in the Catholic Faith. While we continued to live in
Bloomington, Indiana from 1996 to 1998, our family attended
the Lutheran church on Sundays and I attended daily and Sunday Mass at St. Charles Borromeo Church. Life was not easy
as our financial situation continued to be precarious. One of
the greatest joys during this difficult time was the privilege of
working with Marcus Grodi in the Coming Home Network.
Marcus had begun the CHNetwork as an outreach to Protestant clergy like himself — he too had been a Presbyterian minister — as a support and encouragement to other ministers on
the journey to the Church. Since the number of non-Catholic
ministers contacting the CHNetwork was increasing, Marcus
felt that he needed help, and yet he also encouraged me to continue looking into academic positions, as he knew teaching
was close to my heart. He even made arrangements for me
to give a lecture at the Franciscan University of Steubenville,
Ohio where he had worked prior to founding the CHNetwork.

In February of 1998 I received a call from the rector at Holy
Apostles Seminary in Cromwell, Connecticut who was interested in having me come and give a lecture to see whether I

might be a good fit for their seminary faculty. When I visited Holy Apostles I immediately found a great camaraderie with the seminarians. The rector of the seminary was very positive about trying to get me there but, in the end, the seminary was a poor one and did not have the financial resources to pay a layman with a family. My spirits were dashed. I thought it would be a wonderful place to serve God in the Church in a way similar to what I had known at the Reformed Seminary. When I realized that teaching in a Catholic seminary was out of the picture, I sought through prayer to accept God's providence for me and my family.

In May of that same year, I received a call quite unexpectedly from a certain Fr. Stuart Swetland who was the chaplain of the Newman Center at the University of Illinois in Champaign-Urbana. I knew nothing of his name or work. A friend in Bloomington had mentioned my name to a graduate student at the University of Illinois who informed Fr. Swetland of my conversion and past work. Fr. Swetland was an unusually gifted and kind man. He pleaded with me to help him in teaching the Catholic students at the university. After much prayer and discernment, Sharon, our two daughters, and I moved to Champaign-Urbana. Our son, our middle child, had now graduated from high school and had enlisted in the United States Navy.

THE UNIVERSITY OF ILLINOIS, A CATHOLIC DISNEYLAND

My work with the Catholic students at the University of Illinois began one of the most enjoyable and productive periods of my life. Fr. Swetland was as remarkable after I got to know him better as when I knew of him only from a distance. He and the younger priests serving there introduced me to an authentic Catholic life with beautiful liturgies and compassionate service in the confessional. At that time Sharon and our youngest daughter were Lutherans but my wife was now exposed to Catholicism in a new way that broke down some of the cultural barriers she had faced.

In 2001, Monsignor Swetland and I became adjunct professors in the Department of Religion of the University of Illinois. My teaching was a great joy, both because I loved the students and the opportunity it afforded for me to dig more deeply into Catholic theology, especially the Church Fathers. In that same year our oldest daughter Rebekah finished her undergraduate degree at Illinois and was engaged. She and her new husband were married on the Feast of the Queenship of Mary (August 22) in the beautiful campus chapel. It gave my wife and me great joy to see how much her faith had grown.

Around 2002, the newly honored Monsignor Swetland had asked a new women's religious community, the Apostles of the Interior Life, to come and help us in the pastoral ministry to the students. Their impact on the students was nothing short of miraculous. But my wife's new openness to Catholicism was what struck me most. The superior of the Apostles of the Interior Life was a woman named Sr. Susan Pieper, a Californian who had lived in Rome for a number of years. Sharon began taking spiritual direction from Sr. Susan. She couldn't help but be exposed to and influenced by an authentically holy woman.

One of the greatest pleasures of this time was to watch a number of my students find their life vocations. Naturally, most found good Catholic spouses and began their families. Some of my female students discerned their call to religious life while some of the male students went to seminary. My scholarly tendencies were heightened as several of my students went on to academic careers. I thank God from the bottom of my heart that two of my students were ordained into the Apostles of the Interior Life as the first priests of the new Order. Sr. Susan had often asked me to pray that they could begin a male branch of their Order. Little did I realize at the time that some of my own students would enter the male branch. So, it was a great disappointment to me that the Apostles of the Interior Life were asked to leave the campus in 2004. They, being the kindest of women, tried to put the best face on it they could but many students and others felt the loss deeply.

During this same period I was approached by several other universities about teaching in the history of science or liberal studies programs. The most tempting offer came from the University of Notre Dame but, after two on-site visits, both the university and I decided we weren't for one another.

My teaching at Illinois was going famously, but I particularly rejoiced in the hundreds of students who were coming to Mass every day while over three thousand attended on Sundays. I was torn inside. If I had gone to another university where more research was expected, I might have been able to capitalize on the work I had already done and achieved some notoriety in the history of science. Yet, I didn't want to leave the St. John's Newman Center at Illinois because it was, at the time, probably the most effective campus ministry in the country. I wanted to be part of something that nourished both the spiritual and the intellectual life, a beautiful combination fostered by Monsignor Swetland. Life could not have been more wonderful. But clouds were on the horizon.

It was in 2002 that news of the priest abuse scandals in America broke. No matter the positive face we tried to put on this betrayal of priestly trust, faithful clergy and laity of my acquaintance were all reeling from the inner pain of seeing our faith and Church raked over the coals in the media. I was teaching courses on Catholicism in the university, and as I sought to regain composure, another challenge hit me. I didn't know it at the time but the departure of the Apostles of the

Interior Life in 2004 was part of a bigger plan to change things at the Newman Center. In 2006, our new bishop asked Monsignor Swetland — by now more than an employer, a trusted friend — to find some place of service outside the diocese. When he announced his departure, the entire community mourned the loss. As I struggled in the face of this new development, the good Monsignor told me I had to remain to carry on the intellectual apostolate that we had begun together. I felt alone but I knew that there was no other choice.

2010: A YEAR OF PEACE AND TURMOIL

On Easter Vigil of 2010, our son was confirmed and received into the Catholic Church. It was a day of untold joy for me. About two years before, Colin and I began spending more time together, time we had not had while he was serving in the Navy. He had just graduated from Indiana University and was renovating a small house, which he hoped to sell as an investment. Though he lived three hours away, I went to be with him at least once a month. As he worked on the house he had purchased, we had many discussions about the Catholic Church. One day, in the fall of 2009, Colin announced to me that he was going to enter the Rite of Christian Initiation at the same parish that I had been a member of while living in Bloomington. I recall trying to slow him down. I wanted him to make sure that entering the Catholic Church was an informed and prayerful decision. When Sharon and I attended his confirmation on Easter Vigil of 2010, I couldn't help but wonder if this would have an effect on his mother.

During the Easter season that year, our Canadian friend, Marie Jutras, offered to pay for Sharon and me to take a pilgrimage/vacation in Rome. Marie had prayed for years for Sharon that someday she would see fit to join me in my Catholic Faith. Marie knew full well that nothing could force Sharon to become Catholic but she hoped that visiting the center of Christendom might be an encouragement to that end. We had been to Rome twice before. In 2000 during the Great Jubilee, we attended the great Mass of St. John Paul II with our family. At the time only Rebekah and I were Catholics, Sharon and Rachel were Lutheran. Colin, who was living on a Navy base in Sardinia, was Evangelical. In 2003, Sharon and I went on a pilgrimage to Italy with the Apostles of the Interior Life, through the generosity of two very faithful Catholic women. It was a spiritually enriching time and the history of St. Francis in Assisi and the eucharistic miracle in Lanciano had a profound effect on Sharon. Though she never said much, I could tell she was moving closer to the Church in her heart. I think her greatest fear was that of hurting her father who never really understood the Catholic Faith.

In 2010, however, now with two of her children being Catholic, she was becoming bolder. Our many years of prayer and answering questions seem to be paying off. Yet, when we boarded the plane for Rome in June of that year, I was determined not to say anything to her. I only wanted to be there for her, to pray for and with her. We stayed at the Canadian College in Rome and met many new friends from among our noble neighbors to the north. When visiting Assisi, Sharon rediscovered that peace of heart she had experienced when we were there in 2000 and 2003. And in Rome, when we visited various churches, she would ask me questions about this or that structure. When was it built? What was the Christian Faith like at that time? In the end, she was impressed with the deep antiquity of the Church. For me, the night before we were to return to the United States, I was able to spend time in adoration of the Blessed Sacrament with Pope Benedict XVI in St. Peter's Square. In God's providence, we happened to be there during the week of the convocation of priests from all over the world. It was a truly blessed time, a combination of a second honeymoon and a spiritual pilgrimage.

On the plane flight home, Sharon told me that she was ready to become Catholic. Bubbling inside with joy, I quietly asked her why she had come to this decision now. In fact, she had been ready for a long time, but now she came to that point to which every convert to the Church must arrive — the point of no return. For a long time I had known that it was the disappointment such a decision would bring to her father that held her back. Now, she was ready to move ahead. But she asked me again a question she had posed before. Was it necessary for her to tell her father? I told her I would run this by a couple of trusted spiritual advisors but that I didn't think she was under any moral obligation to tell him. In the end, she decided not to tell him.

For Sharon's reception into the Church we didn't want just any priest to officiate for such a special occasion. By now, Monsignor Swetland was serving at Mount St. Mary's University and Seminary in Emmitsburg, Maryland. Occasionally, he returned to the central Illinois area. We arranged that on October 20, 2010, he would be the bishop's agent of Sharon's confirmation.

A few weeks before Sharon and I had gone to Rome in June of 2010, I received an email from the head of our Religion Department asking to meet with me. This was a bit unusual but I was not prepared for what he had to say. He had received an email that I had written to my students in my Introduction to Catholicism class that spring. He was greatly disturbed. Although he had sometimes identified himself as a religious skeptic, he was nevertheless a gracious and helpful man. We had grown into a mutual respect for one another. Some of my students in the past had been his also and they told me that he was always fair. He told me that he respected my intellectual abilities. But even mutual respect could not soften the pain of that conversation. He told me that I could no longer teach in the Department.

When I asked him why, he produced a copy of the email I had written. It was obvious that it was not me as a person that had offended him; it was the content of the email. I had written the email to my students to clarify something left unexplained in my lecture the day before. My lecture had been on homosexuality and explained why the Catholic Church taught that homosexual acts are gravely sinful. I had actually given this lecture for about five years every time I taught that same class. This lecture was the second of two explaining Catholic Moral Teachings, specifically Natural Moral Law. I had come to see that many people, maybe most, have a difficult time understanding the concept of Natural Moral Law. It's not that they understand and disagree; they cannot understand it. But knowing a bit about the development of modern philosophy, I am not surprised. The whole idea is foreign to the thinking of modern people. The meeting that day with the Religion Department head was courteous but unproductive. In an email a few days later he said that he would be glad to work with me on other matters but that the future of my teaching in the Department was settled. I was not allowed to teach. What was I going to do? I was sure that my academic freedom as a professor had been taken away from me; even more disturbing was that my constitutional right of free speech was being violated.

The chancellor of my diocese told me that I had no recourse but to let the matter drop. Even though she was an attorney, I still had my suspicions that she was looking at the matter purely from the standpoint of employment and not from the angle of freedom of speech. I called Monsignor Swetland and he suggested that I contact The Alliance Defending Freedom. After a few consultations with their attorneys, they thought I did indeed have a case. In the meantime, the news of this dismissal hit the media and my former students rallied around me to do what they could. They made a Facebook page called "Save Dr. Ken" and maintained it admirably. Other students contacted media outlets and organized a letter writing campaign to university and diocesan officials. The next few weeks met the new incoming president of the university with a barrage of complaints. Still today, I could not have been prouder of my students. This matter was more than about me. It was an issue of freedom of speech and academic freedom.

All the public pressure — and it was considerable — would not have had any effect on the university if The Alliance Defending Freedom had not been so competent. They sent a letter to the university threatening a lawsuit if they did not reinstate me. As the next few weeks rolled on, several friends on the faculty at Illinois and other places encouraged me to give it up on practical grounds. They were extremely cynical about the university's commitment to the ideals of academic freedom. There was, in their opinion, no way to fight the university. Other faculty members encouraged me to stand firm. And if this matter had been about me as a person, I mostly likely would have given up. But there was much more at stake. Explicitly, this turmoil was about freedom of speech but underneath it was the question of standing up to the powers-that-be for Christ and the Church. During those few weeks in June of 2010 the university was officially silent. And the officials of the diocese were well intentioned but incompetent. The Alliance Defending Freedom urged me to be patient.

After about a month, the attorneys of the Alliance Defending Freedom sent another "demand letter." They threatened a lawsuit if the university did not reinstate me. Within a day or two, I received an official invitation by registered mail, inviting me to teach in the fall semester. I gladly accepted, not out of love for the university, but because I did not want to abandon the students. Yet, even though I told no one at the time, I was sure that this was going to be my last year of teaching at the University of Illinois. I knew that the university officials would maneuver to get rid of me after the 2010-2011 academic year. And that is exactly what they did.

I began laying plans to move on. Part of those plans included the CHNetwork. In 2002, the CHNetwork had begun annual conferences in Columbus, Ohio called Deep in History. I was privileged to be a part of those conferences. Around 2007, I rejoined the staff of the CHNetwork part-time as their Resident Theologian, producing books and articles on various subjects, most especially on the Church Fathers. In 2012, I transitioned to full-time work with the CHNetwork and began both theological and pastoral work. This was very gratifying work because of the quality of my colleagues and because it was such a joy to help searching clergy in their journeys to the Church.

WAS CONVERSION TO THE CATHOLIC CHURCH WORTH IT?

A few years after my confirmation in the Catholic Church, a Protestant friend asked me if converting to Catholicism was worth it. I had asked the same question of a Presbyterian friend who had converted a few years before me. His answer was now mine. I saw myself as Peter who answered for the Apostles in John chapter six. When the crowds abandoned Jesus because of His teaching about the necessity of eating His flesh and drinking His Blood, Jesus asked His own disciples, "You don't want to leave too, do you?" Peter gave an answer as famous as his confession of Jesus as the Messiah in Matthew chapter sixteen. He said to Jesus, "Lord, to whom shall we go? You have the words of eternal life" (Jn 6:68). For someone who truly understands and believes the teachings of the Catholic Church, there is no other choice.

Both are important: understanding and believing. Many well-intentioned Christians and other people of goodwill simply do not understand the Catholic Faith, either in its official teachings or its practices. For some it is a lack of information but for others there are so many misunderstandings that bar the way to faith. It took me a long time to understand the specifics of particular doctrines — and doctrines were important to me — but it took even longer to grasp the underlying assumptions of Catholic thinking.

As I learned more and more of the Catholic Faith, I grew more deeply in my faith but what surprised me was just how rich the Church was in truth, in goodness, and in beauty. The treasures that lie hidden within the Catholic Faith and Church are enormous, more than I could ever have imagined. Early on I used to hear Catholics distinguishing their Faith from Protestantism by calling it *the fullness of Christianity*. Different Protestant churches had various elements of the Catholic Church but no one of them possessed the fullness of them all. By contrast, Catholicism had the full range of all that was good and true. This idea of the fullness of the Christian Faith always struck me because Reformed Christians used to say something similar about their faith. In a spirit of gracious catholicity Calvinists would acknowledge that other forms of Christianity had some value. But it was only the Reformed Faith that was, in the words of Benjamin B. Warfield, a famous Calvinist theologian, "Christianity come into its own." I am sure that faithful Lutherans would have said the same thing about Lutheranism.

What struck me with tornado-like force was just how rich Catholic life and spirituality could be. Eucharistic Adoration and Benediction, the goodness of many diverse vocations from Carthusian silence to active family life, the sheer splendor contained in standard devotions like the Rosary and the Divine Mercy Chaplet, the tender beauty of Marian devotions — all these and more spoke of a living faith that could never be exhausted. Opening the doors of the Catholic Church revealed a treasure trove of gleaming jewels, each shining with spiritual graces in itself but collectively blinding in their brilliance. It is impossible to catalogue them all but I can summarize their substance under four headings. There are treasures of truth, treasures of historical continuity, treasures of union and communion, and treasures of spiritual depth.

One of the things I appreciated most about my Reformed life was the importance of truth. Although all human beings yearn to know what is true, my Presbyterian church life and Reformed theology heightened this human desire in an unusual way. A year after my conversion an old Reformed philosopher friend asked about my becoming Catholic.

"Is it true that you became Catholic?" he asked.

"Yes, it is true" I replied.

With a look of puzzlement, he continued, "But why?"

"The short answer is because I believe it's true."

I could have discussed particular truths with him, but I contented myself with what I still believe. The only compelling reason to become Catholic is the pervasive sense of truth that is embodied in all of Catholicism. Truth can be thought of in at least two ways: correspondence and coherence. I came to believe that Catholicism is true because its philosophy of life corresponds to reality, reality about the world, about human nature, about the Church, but most of all about God Himself. And I came to believe, or rather to see, that the Catholic philosophy of life is a coherent whole, which is life-giving.

In discovering the truths that the Catholic Church teaches, I found myself "deep in history," just as John Henry Newman had said. But there are many people who know something of

Christian history and a few who know a lot. Not everyone, however, views Christian history the same. I discovered that in the Church there was an underlying approach to history that I had long held but rarely articulated, a hermeneutic of continuity. This is the second prominent feature of Catholicism that continually beckons me. Most of the truths we human beings discover have been discovered before. And those that are truly new are still related to and based on earlier truths. This is as true in theology as it is in science, mathematics, and philosophy. The Catholic Church fully recognizes this fact and glories in it. The Catholic ethos seeks to ground itself in the Church Fathers, in the ancient and medieval Church councils, and in the long, arduous process of learning truths from those who have gone before us. The Church is self-consciously in continuity with all that is good and right in Christian history.

Thirdly, in Catholicism, the importance of historical continuity naturally leads to union and communion, or as Chesterton put it, "the democracy of the dead." The idea of union and communion was not foreign to me as a Presbyterian but the Reformed Faith did not possess an underlying metaphysics that could ground the idea and the reality of union and communion. One of the many ways in which Catholicism deepened my life was its richer understanding of the *Communio Sanctorum*. In Presbyterian worship we recited the Apostles' Creed every Sunday so I did indeed believe in the communion of the saints but in the reality of daily life for a Reformed person communion with the saints does not play a large role, if any at all. In Catholic life, if you pray the Rosary daily, you recite the Apostles' Creed and are therefore reminded of this wonderful truth. But it was in the liturgy, in daily Mass, that I came to appreciate the saints as I had never before. Throughout the liturgical year, the Church celebrates various martyrs and other saints who have gone before us marked with the sign of faith (Sign of the Cross). Often in these celebrations we hear prayers like this: "May they [the saints] instruct us by their teaching, and help us by their prayers." Because the saints of the past come from diverse walks of life, they can be models of Christ for us, just as Paul urged in 1 Corinthians 11:1, "Be imitators of me, as I am of Christ."

The phrase in the Creed *Communio Sanctorum* also has another meaning. It can mean not only communion with Christians of the past, it means a sharing in holy things as well. It is a sharing or communion in the lives of those who lived holy lives but also in the holy things they shared in themselves. This is the hope I still carry in my heart, namely, that someday I may be holy too because I now have a share in the same holy realities that they partook of. They devoutly received the Eucharist; they took advantage of the Sacrament of Reconciliation; they devoted significant time to prayer; they nourished their souls on the teachings of Christ and His Apostles; they imbibed the instruction of the saints that preceded them. They increased their holy character — and thus their merits — by selfless giving to those less fortunate than themselves; they valued the things of heaven more than things of the earth.

If I set my heart on these same things and devoted myself to the same truths, I too may someday be holy. That is the promise of the saints. If I draw on the same sources of grace in receiving the Eucharist, in devoting myself to prayer, in sitting at Jesus' feet and hearing His teaching in Scripture, and in a selfless life of love and service, I too can find a level of devotion to God beyond what my human mind can imagine. The saints became saints, not because of what they possessed in themselves, but because of what God's grace was able to do in them with their cooperation. The same possibilities are held out for me.

During my Catholic life the realities of union and communion have been tested and challenged, but through those trials has come a reassurance that I could never live without them. One of my former students used to sign her letters "See you in the Eucharist." This is more than a pious sounding wish. It is a reality of the true Body and Blood of Christ. Through being united to Christ in the Eucharist, I am one with the entire holy, Catholic Church throughout the world. That is worth the world to me.

Perhaps the most wonderful of all the treasures of the Church is its spiritual depth. To the outsider, the Catholic Church appears uniform and even monolithic. But once you step inside, you begin to see a kaleidoscope of spiritualities and devotions that dazzle the eyes of the heart. Desert Fathers, Benedictine, Eastern Monastic, Dominican, Franciscan, Ignatian — all these and more yield a beautiful diversity of ways to live out the gospel. But this variety is also united and bonded to the central truths of the Catholic Faith: Jesus Christ as Redeemer and Lord, the Eucharist as the center of liturgy, and Mary as the Mother of the Church.

My journey into the Church has meant many changes of life and even trials unimaginable when I first began, but I can say without hesitation that I have never looked back. For me, the Catholic Church is my true home, my mother, my Zion. It feeds me with the true Body and Blood of Christ and reconciles me, a sinner, to the Father. Attending and praying at Mass has been one of the deepest joys of my life. The realization that I have access to the very heart of our merciful Jesus through the Sacrament of Reconciliation has been a constant siren beckoning me home. The wisdom of the saints, both theological and spiritual, has ever drawn me into the confidence that what I now believe is not of my own invention but is the faith once and for all delivered to the saints.

✠

About the Author

Kenneth J. Howell is Resident Theologian of the Coming Home Network International. Dr. Howell taught in higher education for almost thirty years, most recently for over a decade as a Professor of Religion at the University of Illinois (Urbana-Champaign) where he taught classes on the history, theology, and philosophy of Catholicism. At the same time he served as the Director of the Institute of Catholic Thought of the St. John's Catholic Newman Center at the same university.

Dr. Howell was a Presbyterian minister for eighteen years and a theological professor for seven years in a Protestant seminary where he taught Hebrew, Greek, and Latin as well as biblical interpretation and the history of Christianity. During his ministry and teaching, Dr. Howell's own reading on the Real Presence of Christ in the Eucharist started him on a six-year journey that eventually led him to Catholicism. On June 1, 1996, Dr. Howell was confirmed and received into the Catholic Church at St. Charles Borromeo Parish in Bloomington, Indiana. In 2000, he received the *Pro Ecclesia et Pontifice* award from John Paul II in recognition of his service to the Church (the lay equivalent of the title Monsignor).

Kenneth Howell has been married to Sharon Canfield for forty years and they have three children. Rebekah, their oldest daughter, lives with her husband, John, in Champaign, Illinois. Their son Colin and his wife live in Rome, Italy. Their youngest daughter Rachel lives in Champaign. They have six grandchildren.

Dr. Howell has authored dozens of articles and seven books: (in reverse order)

1) *Clement of Rome & the Didache: A New Translation and Theological Commentary* (CHResources, 2012)

2) *Ignatius of Antioch & Polycarp of Smyrna: A New Translation and Theological Commentary* (CHResources, 2009)

3) *Questions College Students Ask about God, Faith, and the Church* (Institute of Catholic Thought, 2006)

4) *The Eucharist: A Supper for Lovers* (Catholic Answers Publishing, 2006)

5) *Meeting Mary Our Mother in Faith* (Catholic Answers Publishing, 2003)

6) *God's Two Books: Copernican Cosmology and Biblical Interpretation in Early Modern Science* (University of Notre Dame Press, 2002)

7) *Mary of Nazareth: Sign and Instrument of Christian Unity* (Queenship Press, 1998)